LEAP AHEAD

with

MATHS

Book 7

Brian Nash
Paul Nightingale

Consultant
Brenda Apsley

Illustrated by Jan Wade

NIGHTINGALE PRESS
Devised and produced by Nightingale Press
Unit 5b Causeway Park Industrial Estate, Wilderspool Causeway,
Warrington, Cheshire WA4 6QE England

This edition produced in 1995 for Pegasus Distribution Ltd.,
Unit 5b Causeway Park Industrial Estate, Wilderspool Causeway,
Warrington, Cheshire WA4 6QE England

First published in Great Britain in 1995
by Nightingale Press

Editor Consultant: Brenda Apsley
Illustrator: Jan Wade

Printed in Australia

ISBN 1 - 875288 - 75 - 9

About this book

The most effective learning comes as the result of a three-way partnership between parent, child and teacher in a total learning environment which combines home, school and the outside world. Encouragement, together with repeated practice and investigation will develop skills and confidence, enabling children to get ahead in maths.

The seven books in the series have a revision overlap; thus, the first five units of this book revise and reinforce work covered in Book 6.

Each activity and task is designed to be 'self guiding', but you should offer help when it is needed, explaining concepts and terminolgy. Children should not require close supervision.

Look for opportunities to practise maths. Talk about prices in supermarkets and restaurants, and discuss what discount offers mean. Talk about motorway distance signs and encourage children to become familiar with bus and train timetables and flight times. We are surrounded by maths, so the opportunities are endless!

Key words in maths are printed in **bold** type. Answers are given in the middle of the book, but do not over-emphasise the importance of being 'right' every time. The main objective is in building confidence and understanding.

1.
```
  3481
   652
+ 7036
```

2.
```
  2648
  7906
+  157
```

3.
```
  3841
   762
+ 1309
```

4.
```
   924
  6173
   809
+ 1414
```

5.
```
  6394
    19
   857
+ 5244
```

6.
```
  8061
   329
  9874
+  996
```

7. **3 418** people attended a country show on the first day, **5 657** on the second day and **4 049** on the third day. How many people attended the show altogether? ______

8. A runner covers these distances in four runs: **1 546m**, **2 793m**, **3 468m** and **2 059m**. Write the total in kilometres (decimal notation). ______

9. Pieces of timber measure 1.64m, 2.09m, 3.64m and 2.98m. If these were cut from a single plank, how long was the original plank? ______

10. How many days have you been living? ______

11.
```
  £6549.25
   3072.55
 + 1981.79
```

12.
```
  £9484.21
   8310.85
 + 7426.42
```

Fill in the missing numbers.

13.
```
    30_6
    4598
 + _261
 -------
  14935
```

14.
```
   938_
    6_74
 + 8529
 -------
 _3984
```

15.
```
    7_30
    43_6
 + _87_
 -------
 _1666
```

Draw the **top view** and one **side view** of each **3-D** object.

Top view | Side view

16. 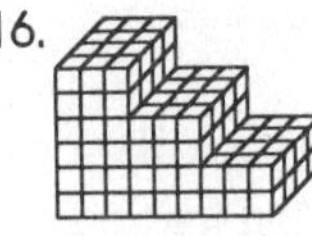

17. 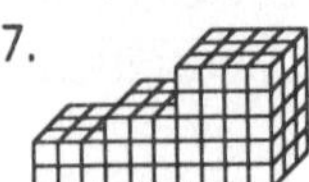

18.

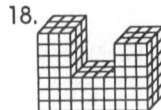

19. Put an **X** on objects that would **stack** well if you had to transport a lot of them.

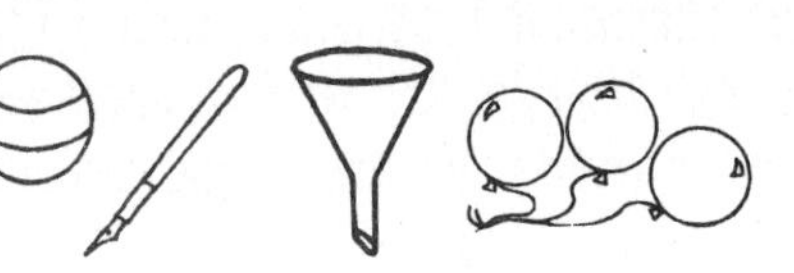

20. If you were going to sell 11 bottles of cooking oil, would you make the bottles **cylindrical** or **rectangular**?

____

21. Why would you choose that shape?

____

____

22. Draw and name the sort of **packaging** you would use to transport these fruits and vegetables.

(a) 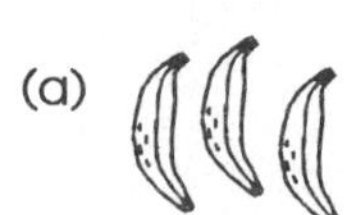 ______

(b) 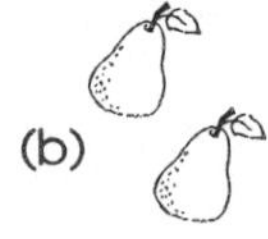 ______

(c) 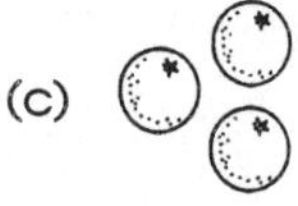 ______

(d)  ______

(d)  ______

1. Convert these **centimetres** to **metres**.

   (a) 650 centimetres = ______________

   (b) 45 centimetres = ______________

   (c) 890 centimetres = ______________

   (d) 164 centimetres = ______________

2. Convert these **metres** to **centimetres**.

   (a) 4 000 metres = ______________

   (b) 3 570 metres = ______________

   (c) 860 metres = ______________

   (d) 1 310 metres = ______________

3. Convert these **metres** to **centimetres**.

   (a) 1.65m = ______________

   (b) 12.03m = ______________

   (c) 8.6m = ______________

   (d) 0.75m = ______________

4. Convert these **kilometres** to **metres**.

   (a) 2.5km = ______________

   (b) 0.45km = ______________

   (c) 17.06km = ______________

   (d) 10.1km = ______________

5. Convert these **distances** to **decimal fractions**.

   (a) $1\frac{1}{2}$ km = ______ . ______ km

   (b) $2\frac{1}{4}$ m = ______ . ______ m

   (c) $4\frac{3}{4}$ m = ______ . ______ m

   (d) $9\frac{1}{2}$ m = ______ . ______ m

   (e) $3\frac{4}{5}$ km = ______ . ______ km

6.
```
  £2716.75
   8093.32
 +  741.03
 _________

 _________
```

7.
```
  £6049.57
    301.10
 + 9860.54
 _________

 _________
```

8. Is icecream usually measured in **litres** or **kilograms**? ________

9. Why do some bottles have hollow bases like this?

____

____

Converting measures to be taught.
100cm = metre.
Dinchy
1000m - Km

…e.

cm
350

… 1 061 at another and **958** at a third. How many photos did they autograph? ________

12. At a Scout jamboree these are the apples that were eaten over four days: **8 930**, **9 986**, **7 524** and **7 061**. How many altogether? ________

Draw the **top view** of each **3-D** object.

13. 

14. 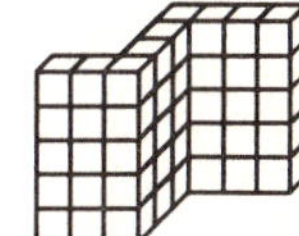

1. 481 − 72 = ______

2. 741 − 23 = ______

3. 538 − 49 = ______

4. 637 − 47 = ______

5. 498 − 79 = ______

6. 887 − 78 = ______

7. 465 − 166 = ______

8. 667 − 88 = ______

9. 975 − 386 = ______

10. **684** people were at the beach on Saturday. On Sunday it rained and there were only **97** people. How many fewer people on Sunday? ______

11. A restaurant had **475** potatoes in the storeroom. If **96** were cut up for chips, how many were left? ______

12. Out of **358** cats at a show, **89** had no tails. How many had tails? ______

13. There were **264** trees lining an avenue. Eighty-five were diseased and were cut down. How many trees left? ______

14. The school cricket team scored **235** runs in a match. Their opponents scored **158** runs. By how many runs did the school win? ______

15. Complete the **subtraction** web.

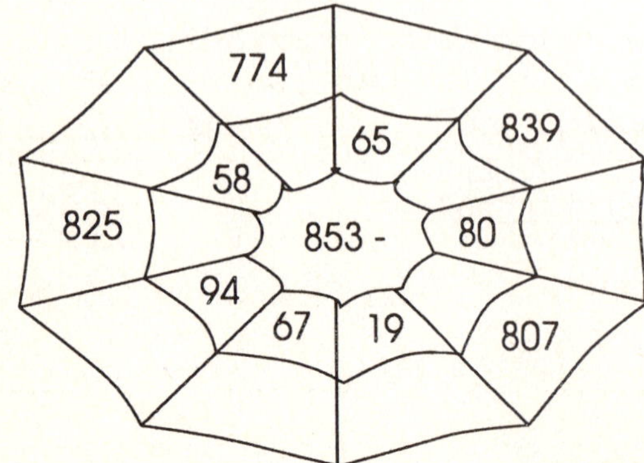

16. Draw the **shadows** formed by this row of trees.

17. Draw the sun in this picture of the tree with **shadow**.

18. Draw a clock on a pillar beside the tree, and show what time it must be.

19. Draw **shadows** for all these objects.

(a)  

(b)  

(c)  

(d)  

(e)   

1. How many **square metres** in one **hectare**? ________

2. How many **hectares** in one **square kilometre**? ________

3. Write these **areas** in **hectares**.

(a) 165 000 m² = ________ ha

(b) 303 500 m² = ________ ha

(c) 19 250 m² = ________ ha

(d) 840 750 m² = ________ ha

4. Write these areas in **square kilometres**.

(a) 400 ha = ________ km²

(b) 1 600 ha = ________ km²

(c) 2 750 ha = ________ km²

(d) 14 250 ha = ________ km²

5. A **hectare** is an **area** 100m x 100m. About how big is the area of land your school stands on? ________

6. What is the **area** of your local sports ground in hectares? ________

7. Find an advertisement in a magazine or newspaper that gives an area in **hectares.** Cut it out and paste it here.

8. Using an atlas or encyclopedia, find the **area** of your county in **km²**.

County	Area in km²
________	________

9. Draw the **shadow** this bus would make under the floodlights.

10. Use a strong light, a white surface and your hand to make funny **shadow** pictures. Draw one here.

11. Write these **areas** in **hectares**.

(a) 630 000 m² = ________

(b) 104 000 m² = ________

(c) 45 750 m² = ________

(d) 10 250 m² = ________

12. 116 − 49 = ________

13. 207 − 78 = ________

14. 463 − 44 = ________

15. 303 − 13 = ________

16. 320 − 13 = ________

17. 676 − 67 = ________

18. 958 − 19 = ________

19. 703 − 87 = ________

20. 741 − 95 = ________

21. 885 − 76 = ________

22. 821 − 39 = ________

23. 471 − 189 = ________

Unit 3

1. 548 − 176 = ____

2. 403 − 274 = ____

3. 762 − 423 = ____

4. 854 − 175 = ____

5. 674 − 576 = ____

6. 346 − 189 = ____

7. 298 − 159 = ____

8. 703 − 444 = ____

9. 861 − 358 = ____

10. Nine hundred and fifty-six people attended a rock concert. **369** had seats. How many had to stand for the concert? ____

11. Complete the **multiplication** web.

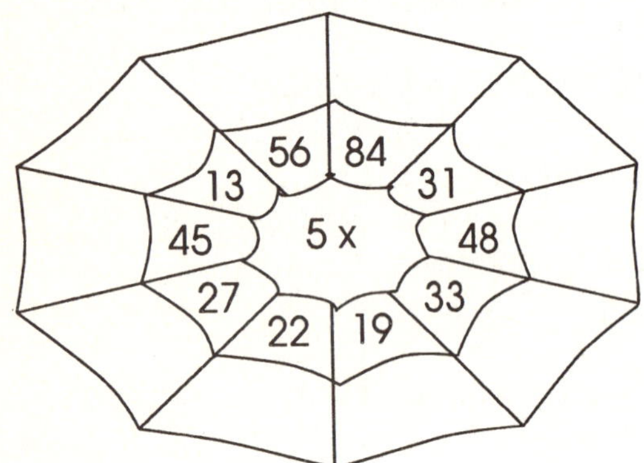

12. 317 x 4 = ____

13. 658 x 7 = ____

14. 745 x 8 = ____

15. 749 x 6 = ____

16. 2789 x 5 = ____

17. 3146 x 4 = ____

18. 1327 x 3 = ____

19. 4158 x 2 = ____

20. 1758 x 8 = ____

21. Continue a line of lamp-posts into the distance along the kerb.

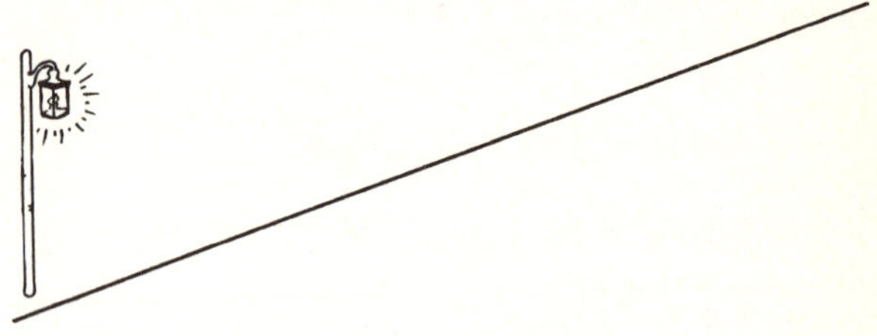

22. Finish this drawing of a house.

23. This hot air balloon is drifting **up** the page to the **right**. Draw how it would appear after several hours.

24. Continue the road and river to a **vanishing point**. Draw another tree in the foreground.

1. With a friend make a model of **one cubic metre**. Use cardboard and tape.

2. Estimate how many times the model will fit into your bathroom at home.

   Volume = ________ m^3

3. Estimate how many cardboard fruit boxes (like the ones apples are packed in) would fit into a **one cubic metre** space. ________

4. List 4 **containers** with capacities given in **cubic metres**.

   ____
   ____
   ____
   ____

5. Can a **cubic metre** be any shape?______

6. What is **gross weight**?

   ____
   ____

7. What is **net weight**?

   ____
   ____

8. Find 3 unopened food containers labelled with **net weight**. Find the **gross weight** and complete the table.

Product	Gross Weight	Net Weight	Weight of packaging

9. Use bathroom scales to find your weight.

   My weight is __________

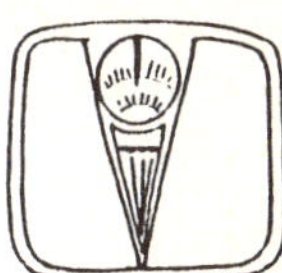

10. $673 - 492 =$ ______

11. $421 - 189 =$ ______

12. $704 - 571 =$ ______

13. $868 - 688 =$ ______

14. $973 - 785 =$ ______

15. $826 - 159 =$ ______

16. Draw a **square metre** on the ground with 3 friends. Stand at the corners and hold a piece of string one **metre** from the ground. You have made **one cubic metre**.

17. How many children could you fit inside the cubic metre? ________

18. If the cubic metre was a different shape, could you fit more people into it ? ________

19. How many could you fit? ________

20. **75** people were seated in a train carriage. How many people if the train has 8 carriages? ________

21. $641 \times 8 =$ ______

22. $1603 \times 6 =$ ______

23. $5607 \times 9 =$ ______

24. Could these children be the same height? Why? ____________

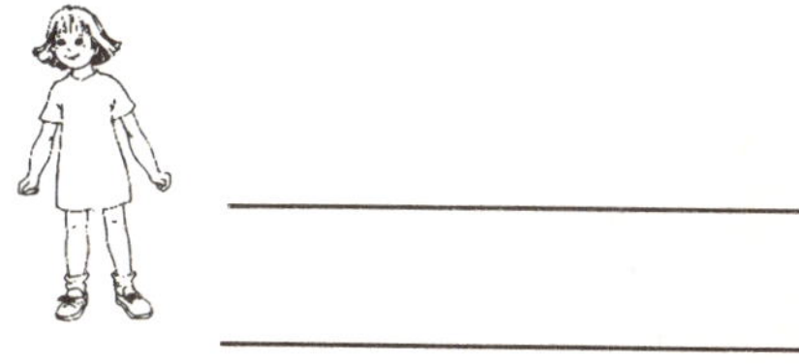

____
____
____

1. 5) 321 r

2. 4) 473 r

3. 3) 262 r

4. 6) 592 r

5. 4) 409 r

6. 7) 381 r

7. 7) 7641 r

8. 5) 5306 r

9. **Divide 392** oranges equally into **7** boxes. How many oranges in each box? ________

10. Plant out **247** seedlings equally into **8** beds.

    (a) How many in each bed? ________

    (b) How many spares? ________

11. **£630** is to be divided equally among **7** bank accounts. How much in each account? ________

12. **481** bales of hay are placed in **8** barns in equal numbers.

    (a) How many bales in each? ________

    (b) How many left over? ________

13. 114 litres of petrol are to be shared among 6 second-hand cars. How many litres in each? ________

14. 8) 6174 r

15. 10) 9132 r

16. 7) 4163 r

17. 5) 2477 r

18. Draw a crossword puzzle pattern by filling in squares in the grid. The result should be a **symmetrical** design.

Fill in: G1 G4 G7 F2 F6 E3 E5 D1 D4 D7 C3 C5 B2 B6 A1 A4 A7

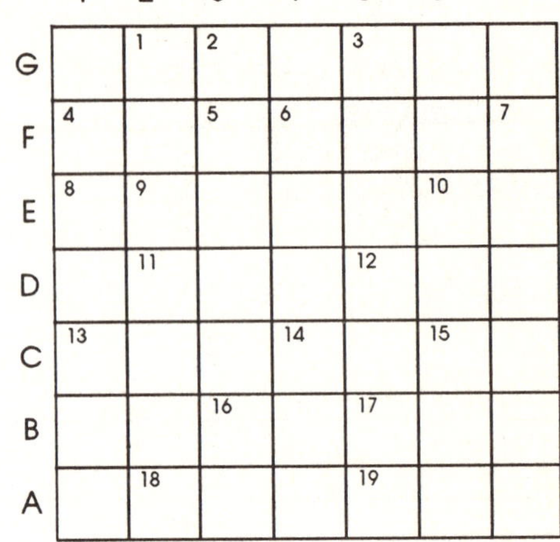

19. List the **co-ordinates** for white squares in columns 2, 4 and 6.

Column 2 ________________________

Column 4 ________________________

Column 6 ________________________

20. Fill in the white squares with numbers and make up a number puzzle. Use addition, subtraction, multiplication and division sums. Write them here.

Across:

1.	12.
3.	13.
5.	15.
8.	16.
10.	18.
11.	19.

Down:

2.	10.
3.	13.
4.	14.
6.	16.
7.	17.
9.	

1. Write the **temperatures** shown on these **thermometers**.

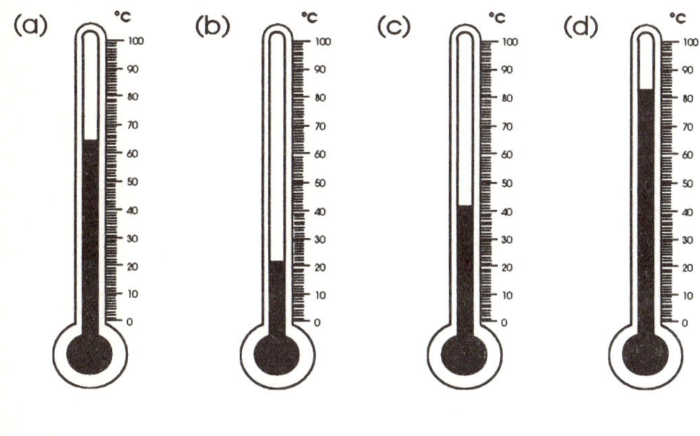

(a) ______ (b) ______ (c) ______ (d) ______

2. Use a coloured pen to show these **temperatures** on the **thermometers**.

(a) °C (b) °C (c) °C

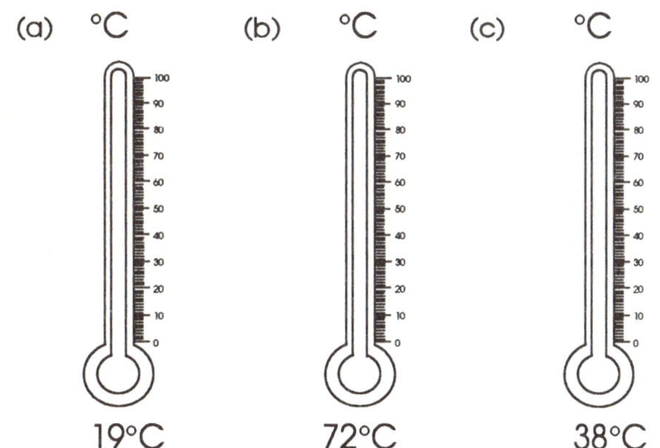

19°C 72°C 38°C

3. Circle the highest **temperature** reading.

18°C 43°C 19°C 27°C 22°C

4. Circle the lowest **temperature** reading.

23°C 34°C 19° 9°C 29°C

5. On a separate piece of paper, make a **graph** to show these **temperature** readings during a day.

8:00 a.m.	14°C	2:00 p.m.	25°C
10:00 a.m.	17°C	4:00 p.m.	21°C
noon	22°C	6:00 p.m.	18°C

6. At a base in the Antarctic, the **temperature** varies between -32°C and 17°C. What is the **temperature range**? ______

7. A path **920 metres** long is **divided** into **eight** lengths. How many metres in each length? ______

8. **498 grams** of butter is to be divided equally for **six** cakes. How many grams per cake? ______

9. 7)4 390 r

10. 9)5 038 r

11. 8)3 714 r

12. 5)8 784 r

13. 6)7 651 r

14. 9)1 171 r

15. What is the **temperature** shown on the **thermometer**? ______

16. Add to the shading so the temperature reads 45°C.

17. What is the difference between the original reading and 45°C? ______

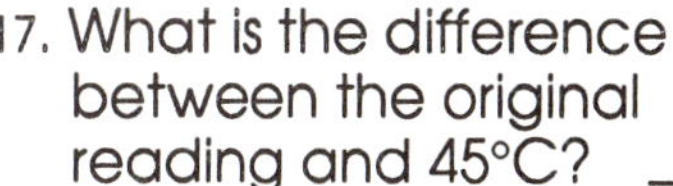

18. What is the difference in **temperature** between -1°C and 1°C? ______

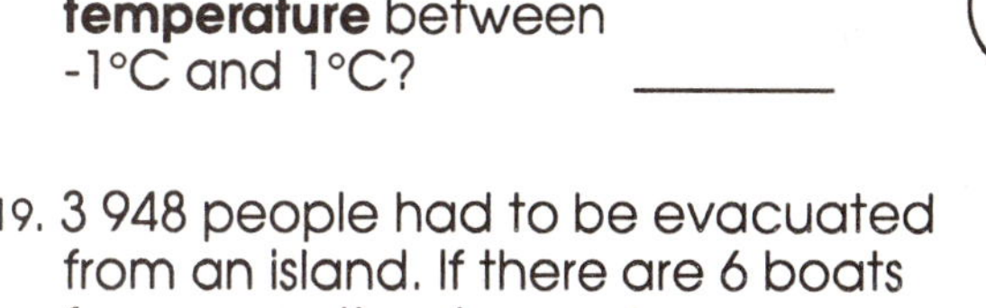

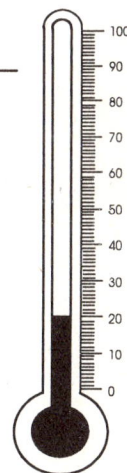

19. 3 948 people had to be evacuated from an island. If there are 6 boats for evacuation, how many people on each boat? ______

20. **Nine** people won a lottery prize of **£10 000**. How much will they each receive in whole pounds? ______

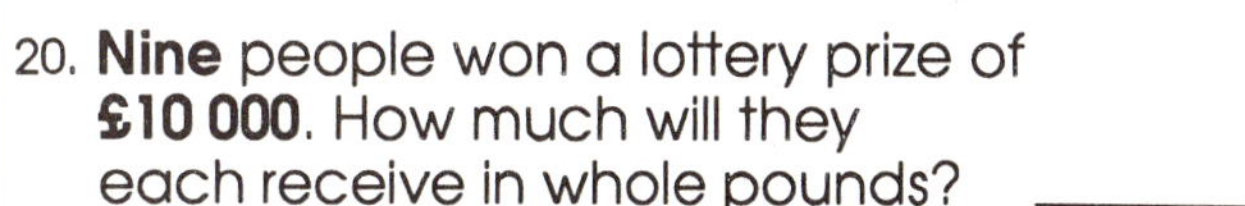

21. How much is left over? ______

22. Suggest what they could do with the money left over.

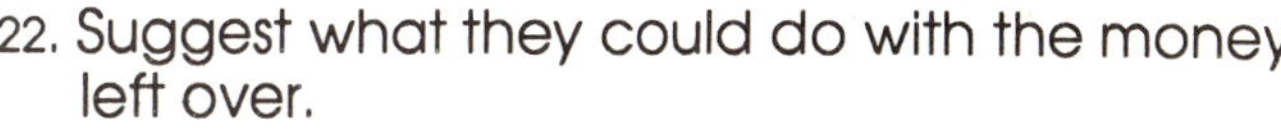

______

______

Place each set of **fractions** in order smallest to largest.

1. 0.9 1.65 0.8 2.65 1.63 2.62

____

2. 2.07 2.70 2.17 2.71 2.77 2.27

____

3. 3.65 4.40 2.64 3.56 4.04 2.46

____

4. 6.79 9.76 7.9 6.97 9.67 7.09

____

5. Write each of these **fractions** without the **non-significant** (not needed) **zeros**.

(a) 0.860 _______ (b) 10.30 _______

(c) 3.10 _______ (d) 03.01 _______

(e) 10.050 _______ (f) 8.06 _______

6. Write these amounts in pounds using **decimal notation**.

(a) 2 730p _______ (b) 6 849p _______

(c) 30p _______ (d) 9 362p _______

(e) 250p _______ (f) 5p _______

7. Write these lengths in **metres** using **decimal notation**.

(a) 314cm _______ (b) 90cm _______

(c) 868cm _______ (d) 750cm _______

(e) 1 268cm _______ (f) 2 035cm _______

Add **375** to each of these numbers.

8. 6 259 _______ 9. 7 167 _______

10. 3 978 _______ 11. 4 989 _______

12. Write the numbers 85 less than:

(a) 6 471 _______ (b) 6 114 _______

This **graph** shows the highest monthly **temperatures** in Hotsville from July to December.

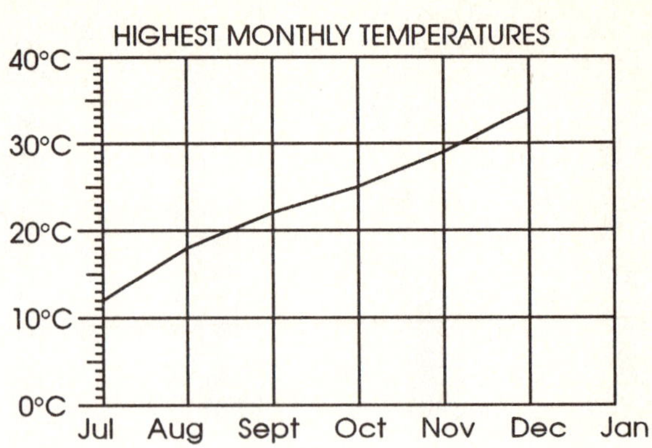

13. What was the highest **temperature** in August? _______

14. What was the highest **temperature** in December? _______

15. What is the general trend of the **graph**?

____

16. What is the **temperature** range of the **graph**? _______

17. In January the **temperature** reached 38°C. Fill this in and continue the graph.

*This **pie chart** shows popular holiday destinations. About **200 000** people travelled overseas in the year shown.*

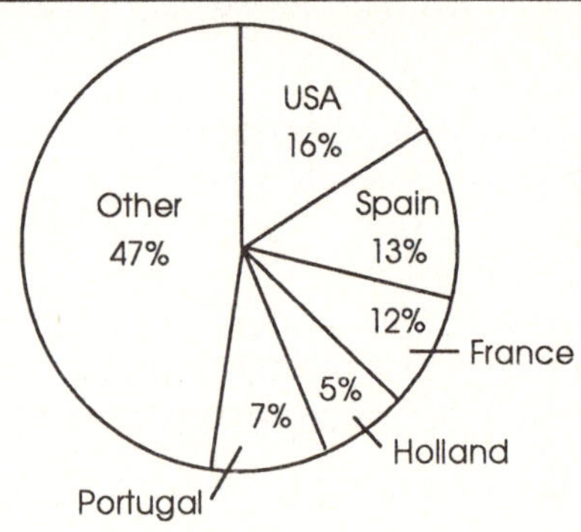

18. How many travelled to the USA? _______

19. How many to Spain? _______

20. How many to Holland? _______

21. How many to Portugal? _______

22. How many to France? _______

1. Add hands to the **analog stopwatches.**

(a)

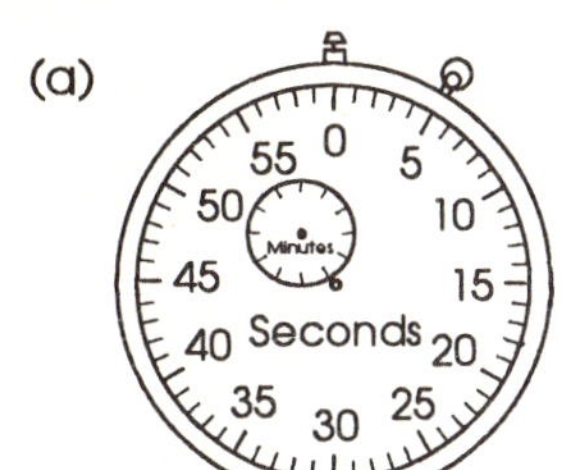

2 minutes and **15** seconds

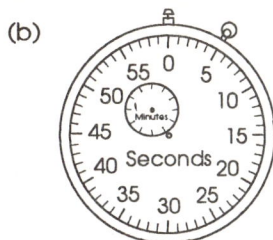

(b)

9 minutes and **47** seconds

(c)

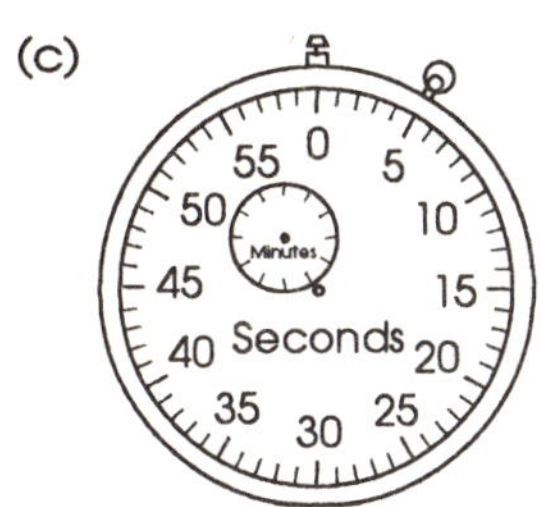

4 minutes and **23** seconds

(d)

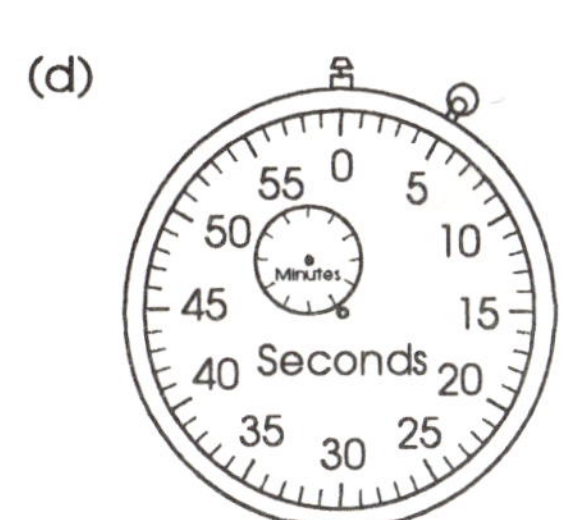

6 minutes and **56** seconds

2. Show times on the **digital stopwatches.**

(a)

4 minutes **9** seconds and **33** hundredths

(b)

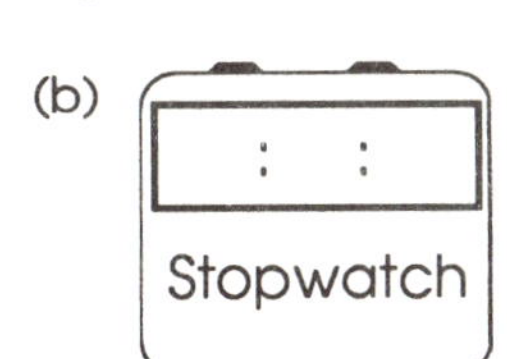

7 minutes **46** seconds and **5** hundredths

3. Using a **stopwatch**, find out how long it takes you to write the whole alphabet. ________

4. Using a **stopwatch**, find out how long it takes to jog to the local shops and back. ________

5. Set a **stopwatch** going and hold it where you can't see it. Stop it when you think $2\frac{1}{2}$ minutes has passed. Do this three times and record the results.

Estimate	Time	Difference + or -
1st reading		
2nd reading		
3rd reading		

6. Write these numbers leaving out the **non-significant zeros.**

(a) 09.4 ________ (b) 10.06 ________

(c) 0.303 ________ (d) 8.10 ________

(e) 07.50 ________ (f) 3.020 ________

7. Record the readings on these **analog stopwatches.**

(a)

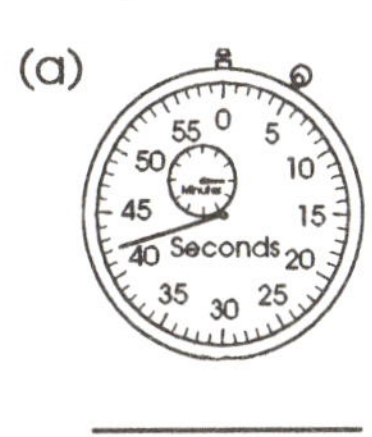

____

____

(b)

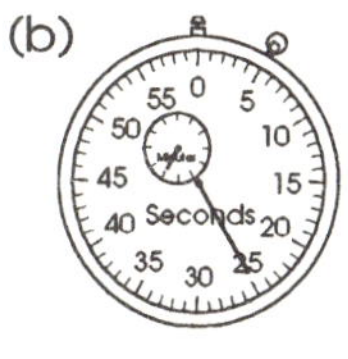

____

____

(c)

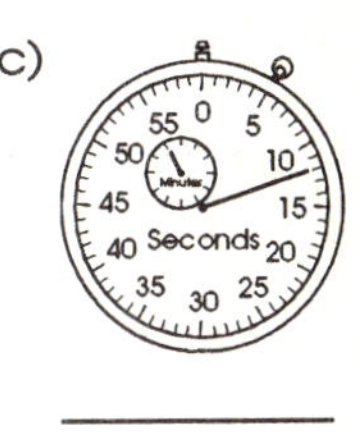

____

____

8. Record the readings on these **digital stopwatches.**

(a)

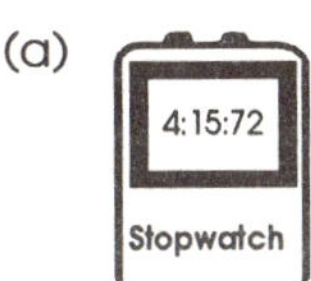

____

____

____

(b)

____

____

____

(c)

____

____

____

9. Write these **fractions** in order - largest to smallest.

9.06 7.62 4.93 9.6 3.49 6.94

____

10. Change these amounts into pence.

(a) £7.80 ________ (b) £1.09 ________

(c) £19.75 ________ (d) £14.44 ________

11. If a computer game costs **£29.95**, how much will **6** cost? ________

12. How many hundredths between **8.76** and **8.89**? ________

13. A stopwatch records that a car completed a race in 4 minutes, but the stopwatch runs 5 seconds slow each minute. How long did the car really take to complete the race? ________

Write these numbers in words.

1. 18 365 ______

2. 64 201 ______

3. 32 798 ______

4. 40 572 ______

Write these words as numbers.

5. Fifty-one thousand four hundred and thirty-three ______

6. Forty-seven thousand one hundred and ninety-six ______

7. Sixteen thousand seven hundred and sixty-four ______

8. Ninety thousand nine hundred and ninety-nine ______

Identify the **value** of numbers in bold, ten thousand, thousand, hundred, ten or unit.

9. 8**2** 657 ______

10. 40 71**3** ______

11. **7**9 909 ______

12. 64 **4**20 ______

Write these numbers in rising order.

13. 16 497   59 023   15 981   59 076   58 470

______

14. 66 701   66 017   66 710   66 007   66 717

______

15. 90 919   91 901   90 009   91 909   90 900

______

16. Complete the table of **metres (m), centimetres (cm)** and **millimetres (mm).**

m	cm	mm
	70	
		350
4.0		
	1 750	

m	cm	mm
1.6		
		2 350
	7	
		98

17. Complete this table **of metres (m)** and **kilometres (km).**

m	km
1 200	
	5.0
3 840	
	9.625
2 078	
	11.301

18. Look at an atlas or road map, and record four distances in km.

From	To	km

19. It is 85km from Harper to Lincoln, and 105km further to Billings. What is the distance from Harper to Billings? ______

20. Find how far you live from London in a direct line. ______

21. Find out about 'old' measures of length like miles. It is 185 miles from London to Manchester. How many km? ______

1. Add 100 000 to 749 632 ____________

2. Add 200 000 to 406 544 ____________

3. Add 150 000 to 580 721 ____________

4. What number is 100 000 less than 892 184? ____________

5. Write the number 200 000 less than 647 039 ____________

6. Write the number 150 000 less than 532 165 ____________

7. Write this list of numbers in order from smallest at the top.

   432 671 ______________

   715 609 ______________

   340 118 ______________

   304 811 ______________

   751 960 ______________

   304 810 ______________

Write these words as numbers.

8. Seven hundred and three thousand, eight hundred and forty-three ________

9. One hundred and eleven thousand one hundred and ten ________

10. Four hundred and ten thousand, five hundred and seventy-one ________

11. Twenty-nine thousand two hundred and seven ________

12. Write these numbers in words.

   (a) 631 492 ______________________________

   ____

   (b) 206 583 ______________________________

   ____

13. Write five hundred and twenty-seven thousand six hundred and seventy-eight in numbers. ________

14. Write 261 409 in words.

   ____

   ____

Change these **kilometres** to **metres.**

15. 8.3km ________

16. 7.962km ________

17. 13.504km ________

18. 11.697km ________

19. 0.45km ________

20. Complete the table.

cm	m	km
	525	
1 278		
	72	
		9.34

21. Find how far it is from where you live to Edinburgh in a straight line. ________

22. Write the **Roman numerals** for these numbers.

1	________	100	________
5	________	500	________
10	________	1 000	________
50	________	2 000	________

23. Add 250 000 to 16 394 ________

24. Add 75 000 to 231 616 ________

25. Take 100 000 from 716 271 ________

26. Take 350 000 from 816 161 ________

Unit 7

1.
```
 731
  24
+156
```

2.
```
  39
 312
+143
```

3.
```
 691
 178
+250
```

4.
```
  784
  173
  245
+ 306
```

5.
```
  502
   98
  326
+  71
```

6.
```
  813
    9
  267
+  35
```

7.
```
 £127.35
  456.72
 +159.37
```

8.
```
 £216.43
  718.15
+  91.96
```

These are the results of a cricket competition.

Cricket Results

Brooke	**138**	*defeated*	Headland	**127**
Seaview	**297**	*defeated*	Fernley	**186**
Wimbush	**306**	*defeated*	Turville	**229**
Glossop	**213**	*defeated*	Harper	**133**

9. Add the winning scores ________

10. Add the losing scores ________

11. Add the scores over 200 ________

12. Add the scores below 200 ________

13. Add all the scores together ________

Fill in the missing numbers in these addition sums.

14.
```
 342
 261
+118
 7_1
```

15.
```
 60_
 _24
+ 89
 816
```

16.
```
 51_
 _67
+295
 9_2
```

17. List three **packing materials** that are used to stop things moving around when they are transported.

____

____

____

18. Colour the objects that would need a **packing** material if they were transported in a **rectangular** box.

   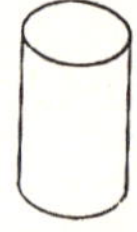 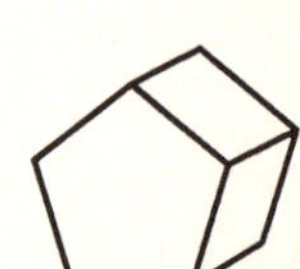

19. List three household items that usually come **packed** in polystyrene.

____

____

____

20. Why are drinking cups usually **round** instead of **square?**

____

____

21. Why are underground pipes **cylindrical?**

____

____

22. There are signs used on boxes to indicate something is **fragile,** and boxes should be kept **right way up.** Draw the signs here.

1. Convert these distances to **decimal notation**.

(a) 2km 720m = ________

(b) 7km 845m = ________

(c) 15km 503m = ________

(d) 11km 107m = ________

(e) 19km 99m = ________

This is a map of a seaside resort.

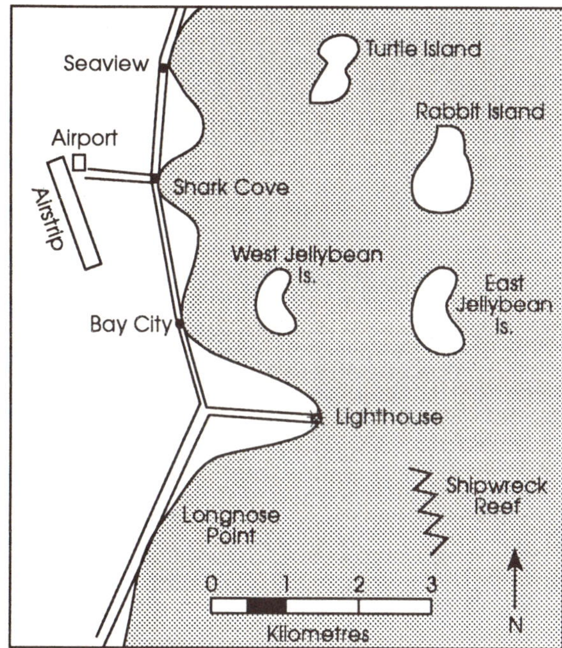

2. How far is it by road from Shark Cove to Bay City? ________

3. How far by road from the airport to the lighthouse? ________

4. How long is the airstrip? ________

5. How far by boat from Shark Cove to East Jellybean Is.? ________

6. How far from Seaview to Shipwreck Reef and return by boat? ________

7. How far would you travel by helicopter from the airport to Turtle Is., to East Jellybean Is., to the lighthouse, to West Jellybean Is. and then back to the airport? ________

These items are on display at a toy shop.

8. How much would the pram, helicopter and ball cost? ________

9. Add the prices of the train, helicopter and guitar. ________

10. Add the prices of the teddy bear, train and marbles together. ________

11. Write the answers 8 - 10 to the nearest whole pound.

1. ________ 2. ________ 3. ________

12. A family travels by camper van for three days and covers 364km, 419km and 326km. How far altogether? ________

13. Give an example where springs are used so something being carried is not damaged by bumps.

____

14. Where is a liquid used for a similar purpose?

____

15.	16.	17.
349	871	4713
604	346	265
723	175	9
+ 158	+ 258	+ 1718
________	________	________

Give the Roman numerals for:

18. 20 ________ 19. 60 ________

20. 300 ________ 21. 900 ________

1.
```
 7648
+3912
```

2.
```
 4063
 6178
+ 341
```

3.
```
 5687
 2041
 6293
+4326
```

4.
```
 7380
  927
 5834
+  89
```

5.
```
 9034
  793
 8671
+ 825
```

6.
```
 7156
 4382
 7005
+  99
```

7. Add the last four years of rainfall for Harper: 1 237mm, 964mm, 1 198mm and 1 306mm. ______

8. A small business made profits over four years: £2 467, £3790, £7 981 and £6 482. What was the total profit? ______

9. A long-distance lorry travels these distances in five trips: 7 948km, 984km, 5 756km, 1 093km and 2 710km. How many kilometres altogether? ______

10. 3 612 + 4 805 + 1 792 + 2 539 = ______

Find the total and make up a number story to fit this sum.

______

______

______

Use a calculator to add these numbers.

11. 2 490 + 3 560 + 4 510 = ______

12. 7 364 + 6 789 + 2 035 = ______

13. 3 459 + 7 602 + 1 861 = ______

14. 6 730 + 3 482 + 788 = ______

Count the **total** number of cubes in each **3-D** group and the number of cubes that can't be seen.

	3-D Objects	Total Cubes	Unseen Cubes
15.			
16.			
17.			

Show the number of dots on the opposite side of each die.

18. 19.

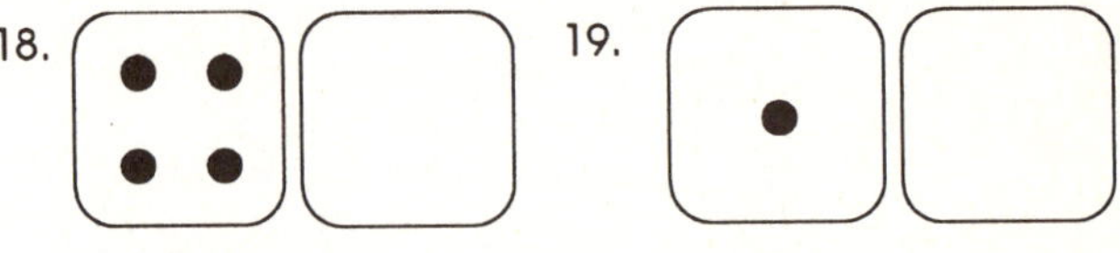

20. 21.

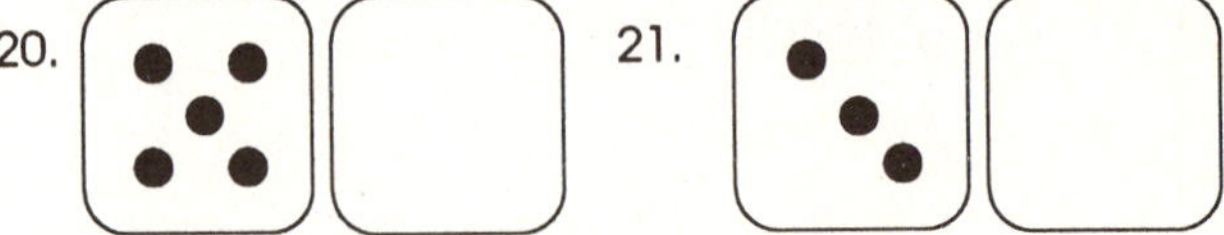

22. What is the sum of the opposite sides of a die? ______

23. Draw the two shapes needed to make this shape a complete cube.

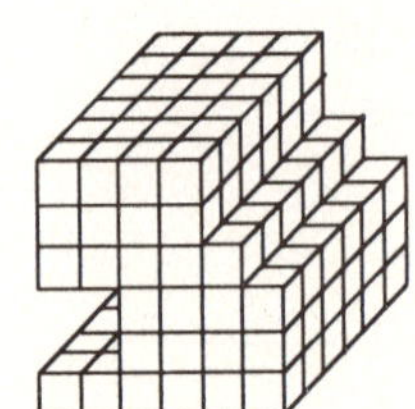

Write these **areas** as **hectares.** The first one is done for you.

1. 60 500 square metres **6.05 ha**
2. 15 000 square metres ______
3. 27 500 square metres ______
4. 5 500 square metres ______
5. 12 750 square metres ______

Which unit of area would you use in measuring these?

6. The floor area of your home ______
7. The Kalahari Desert ______
8. A page of this book ______
9. The top of your desk ______
10. Floor of an aircraft hangar ______
11. A railway station ______
12. The area of the English Channel ______
13. An area of three **hectares** has been set aside for a football stadium. Would this be enough? ______
14. One **square kilometre** has been set aside for an international airport. Does this seem enough? ______
15. **100m^2** of carpet has been ordered for a family-sized home. Could this be right? ______
16. List four areas that measure about one hectare.

    (a) ______

    (b) ______

    (c) ______

    (d) ______

Use a calculator to add these.

17. £2 560 + £3 420 + £1 486 = ______
18. £4 280 + £1 760 + £1 925 = ______
19. 1 763km + 2 424km + 2 875km = ______
20. 3 420km + 3 999km + 3 514km = ______
21. 2.635kg + 4.315kg + 3.891 kg = ______
22. Write these **hectares** as **square metres.**

    (a) $1\frac{1}{2}$ha ______

    (b) $4\frac{1}{4}$ha ______

    (c) 3.825ha ______

    (d) 2.175ha ______

    (e) 5.333ha ______

23.
```
  6132
  4927
  3206
 +2005
 -----
```

24.
```
  9302
  7816
  5967
 + 340
 -----
```

25.
```
  2006
   612
  2026
 +6267
 -----
```

26.
```
  8342
  7854
  3917
 +2648
 -----
```

27.
```
  1348
  9610
    67
 + 315
 -----
```

28.
```
  2475
  3167
   258
 +   7
 -----
```

29. A school paid £4 372 for 6 computers, £3 756 for copying paper, £2 704 for sporting gear and £563 for a refrigerator. What was the school's total payment? ______
30. How many dots are on the opposite side to the six on a die? ______
31. Add three more numbers to this sequence.

    3 4 5 6 8 10 9 12 15 ___ ___ ___

1. 431
 -267

2. 359
 -176

3. 580
 -301

4. 676
 -358

5. 893
 -404

6. 974
 -787

7. 621
 -339

8. 415
 -239

9. 701
 -503

10. $225m^2$ of carpet is ordered for a school hall. Only $187m^2$ is used. How much left over? ________

11. A weekend car rally is **946km**. If cars complete **476km** on the first day, how many kilometres are to be covered on the second day? ________

12. It is **183** days to Jade's eleventh birthday and **269** days to Erin's eleventh birthday. What is the difference in their ages? ________

13. Who is older? ________

14. A weekend for a family at the Ritz Hotel costs **£347.** At the Tullymore Guest House a weekend costs **£129.** How much would you save by staying at the Tullymore? ________

15. Chantry Flats has a population of **823;** Bridgehill has a population of **409.** How many people would have to move from Chantry to Bridgehill to make the populations equal? ________

16. Draw these four types of angles and label them: **obtuse, right angle, reflex** and **straight.**

(a) (b)

(c) (d)

17. Measure these angles, using a **protractor.**

(a)

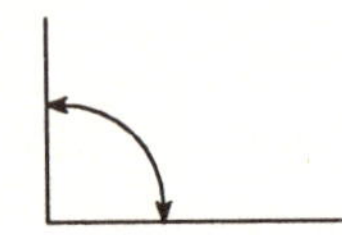

____

(b)

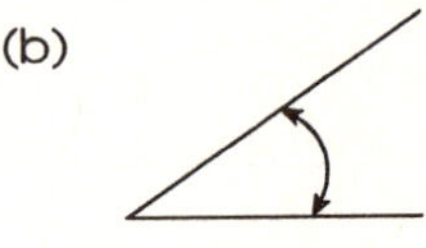

____

(c)

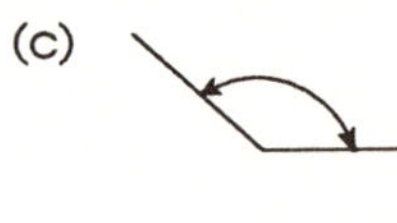

____

(d)

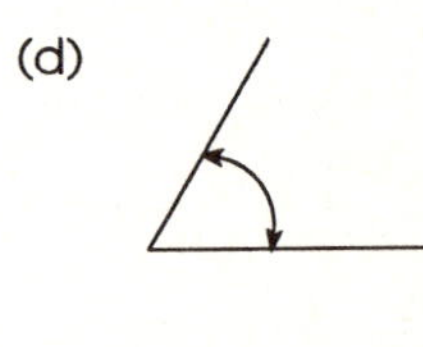

____

18. Draw angles of **45°**, **85°** and **150°** using a protractor. Label each one.

19. Draw and label a **60°** angle at the centre of this circle, then a **140°** angle and an **80°** angle next to that. Measure the angle that is left.

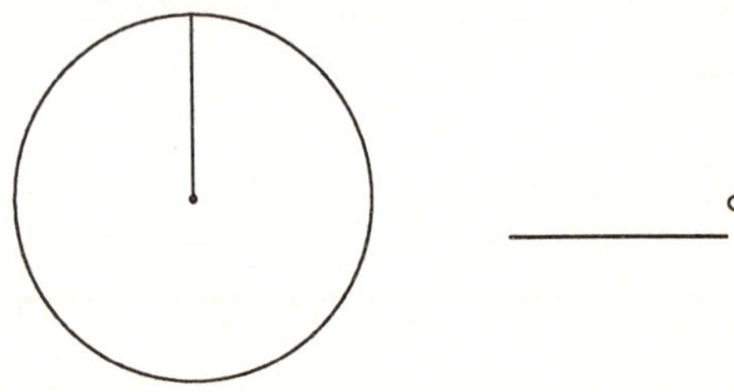

________°

20. What is the sum of the angles in the circle? ________

Complete these subtraction sums.

1.
```
  747
 -358
 ----
 __89
```

2.
```
  809
 -763
 ----
  __6
```

3.
```
  67__
 -323
 ----
  348
```

4.
```
  9__2
 -603
 ----
 __89
```

5.
```
  88__
 -__37
 ----
  448
```

6.
```
  7__9
 -334
 ----
  38__
```

7.
```
  66__
 -6__9
 ----
   12
```

8.
```
  __64
 -5__7
 ----
  33__
```

9.
```
  9__1
 -__93
 ----
  48__
```

10. A tanker contains **473l** of water. **131l** of liquid fertilizer is added and **206l** of the mixture is used. How much of the mixture is left? ________

11. A woman has **£785** to spend. She buys a camera for **£187** and a video for **£236.** How much is left? ______

12. Ahmed spent **117** days in hospital over two years. How many days was he out of hospital? *(One year was a leap year.)* ________

13. Complete the subtraction sum. Then make up a story to go with it.

____

____

____

____

```
  831
 -645
 ----
 ____
```

14. Take the numbers in the side row from those in the top to complete the table.

–	627	485	711	943
258				
197				

Use a **protractor** to draw these angles.

15. 30°

16. 15°

17. 120°

18. 165°

19. Measure these angles and name them.

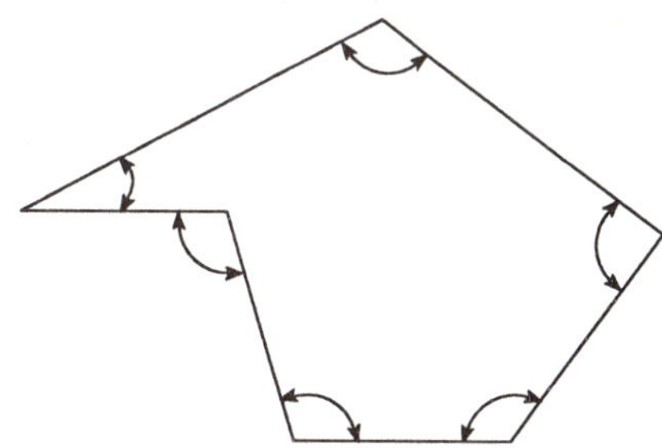

20.
```
  694
 -427
 ----
```

21.
```
  975
 -887
 ----
```

22.
```
  £804
 -£749
 -----
```

23.
```
  £998
 -£989
 -----
```

24.
```
  675km
 -197km
 ------
```

25.
```
  492km
 -135km
 ------
```

26. Write these Roman numerals as numbers.

(a) XXX ________ (b) CX ________

(c) LII ________ (d) XV ________

(e) DC ________ (f) CMI ________

1. 361 x 2

2. 425 x 4

3. 709 x 5

4. 658 x 6

5. 548 x 7

6. 832 x 8

7. 464 x 9

8. 671 x 7

9. 309 x 6

10. Calculate the **answers,** and fill in the cross number puzzle.

Across	Down
1. 7 x 28 =	1. 4 x 41 =
3. 7 x 45 =	2. 2 x 47 =
6. 8 x 8 =	4. 2 x 24 =
8. 2 x 40 =	5. 4 x 127 =
9. 6 x 102 =	7. 9 x 9 =
11. 9 x 5 =	9. 4 x 163 =
12. 5 x 7 =	10. 8 x 29 =
14. 4 x 63 =	13. 7 x 104 =
17. 3 x 9 =	15. 8 x 7 =
19. 6 x 8 =	16. 4 x 172 =
20. 7 x 124 =	18. 4 x 19 =
21. 8 x 111 =	19. 6 x 8 =

11. A plane carries **347** passengers when full. If **8** full planes leave Glasgow, how many passengers? ________

12. A hall can seat **897** people. The hall was booked for **6** concerts which were all full houses. How many people saw the concert? ________

13. A party of mountaineers plans to set up six camps on Mt Danger. Using the co-ordinates, mark each camp.

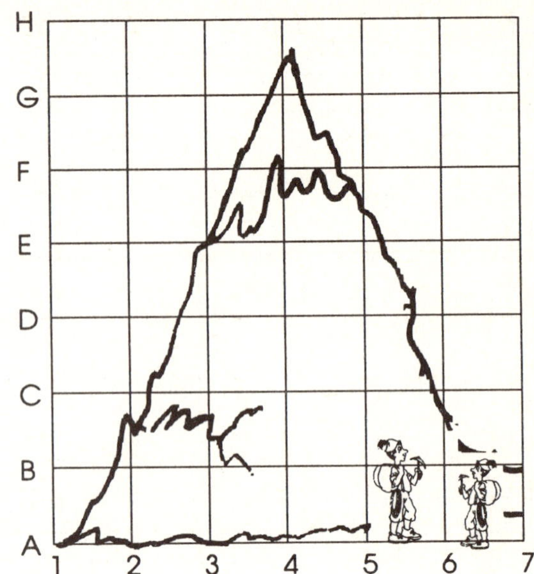

Base Camp ***B2*** *Camp 1* ***C3*** *Camp 2* ***D4***
Camp 3 ***E3*** *Camp 4* ***F5*** *Camp 5* ***G4***

14. At a poultry farm, this was the egg production for a week.

Sunday 115	*Thursday 120*
Monday 150	*Friday 135*
Tuesday 175	*Saturday 120*
Wednesday 140	

Plot these figures on the grid, and join the points to show how production varies.

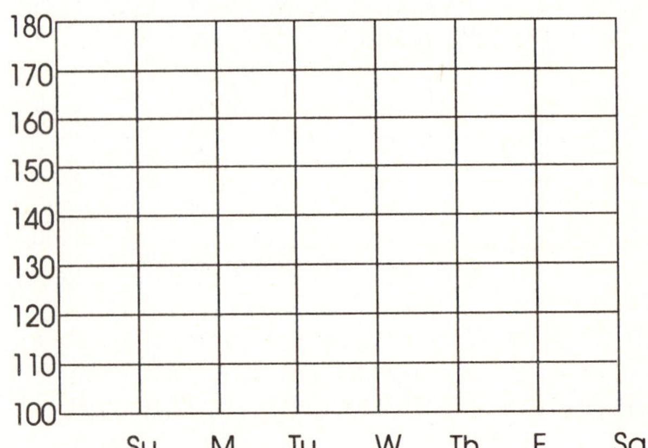

15. How many eggs were produced over the full week? ________

Select and measure the **weight** of ten objects to the nearest **gram.** Don't select anything more than **4kg.**

	Object	Weight
1.		
2.		
3.		
4.		
5.		
6.		
7.		
8.		
9.		
10.		

11. Using rice and kitchen scales measure out these **weights.** Ask a friend to check your measurements, and tick each as you complete it.

(a) 25g Tick ☐ (b) 130g Tick ☐

(c) 96g Tick ☐ (d) 250g Tick ☐

List the smallest number of **standard weights** (1kg, 500g, 200g, 100g, 50g, 20g, 10g, 5g and 1g) needed to **measure** these amounts.

12. 2.497kg ______________________

13. 1.248kg ______________________

14. 520g ______________________

15. 634g ______________________

16. A clever inventor invented this 'itchy' T-shirt. You tell someone where you are itchy and they scratch you. Mark these itchy spots with an X.

A3 F9 D6 C8 H4 J10

17. 9 x 301 = ______ 18. 8 x 647 = ______

19. 7 x 588 = ______ 20. 6 x 932 = ______

21. 9 x 715 = ______ 22. 8 x 572 = ______

23. Write these **grams** as **kilograms,** using **decimal fractions.**

(a) 792g ______ (b) 2 380g ______

(c) 4 821g ______ (d) 5 060g ______

24. List the smallest number of **standard** weights needed to measure a weight of 2.531kg.

____

25. Complete the **multiplication** web.

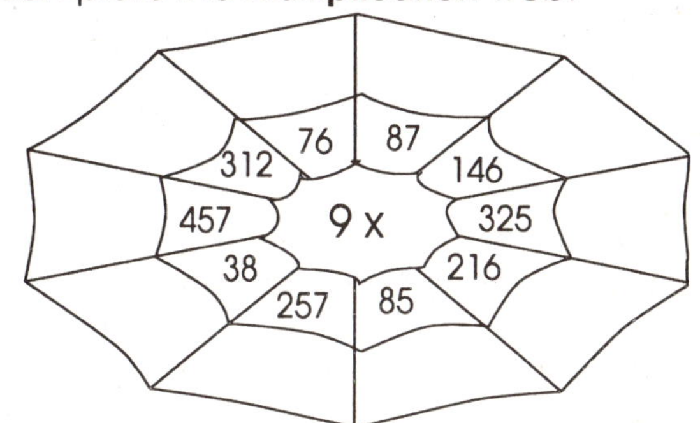

1. 1762 x 2 = ______
2. 2413 x 3 = ______
3. 8015 x 8 = ______
4. 7136 x 4 = ______
5. 6436 x 7 = ______
6. 3404 x 6 = ______
7. 4351 x 5 = ______
8. 2219 x 9 = ______
9. 3978 x 7 = ______

10. An electrical shop advertised TVs and videos for **£1 049** and sold **7** in one day. What did the sales total? ______

11. The same store advertised fridge freezers at **£986** each and sold **9** on the same day. What did these sales total? ______

12. What were the total sales for TVs and videos and fridge freezers on the day? ______

13. A public library lends an average of **2 780** books each week for **8** weeks. How many books loaned altogether? ______

14. Nine houses are built on a new estate and each requires **3 875** roof tiles. How many tiles needed altogether? ______

15. A plumber estimates a school wastes **1 654l** of water each week from leaking taps. How much in **9** weeks if he did not fix the taps? ______

16. Complete the **multiplication** table.

x	635	179	836	217	473
8					

This is a map of Clinton.

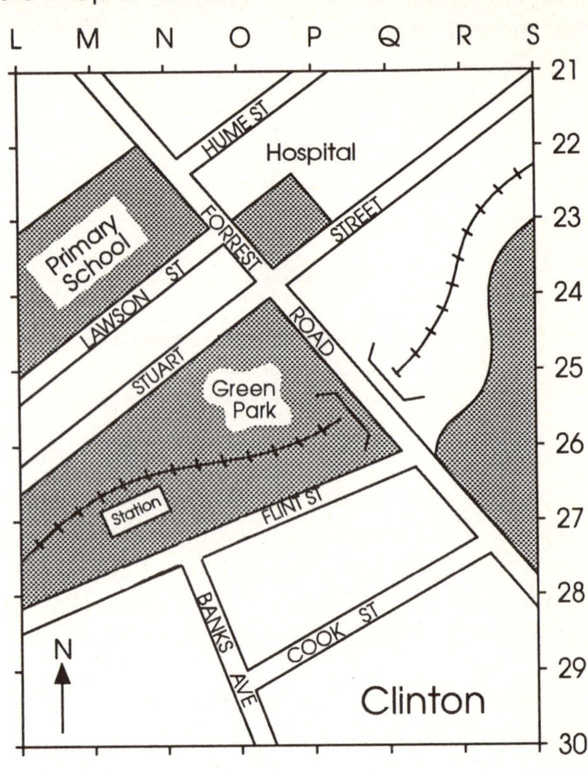

17. Draw the cross-reference lines on the map of Clinton, using a coloured pencil.

18. Give the **street** references for the hospital.

______ ______

19. Give the co-ordinates for the railway station. ______

20. Give co-ordinates for the corner of Flint St and Banks Ave. ______

21. Give co-ordinates for the point where Lawson St goes off the map. ______

22. Give the street intersection and the co-ordinates for the eastern corner of the Primary School grounds.

______ ______ ______

23. What are the co-ordinates for the bridge over the railway? ______

24. Find a good place for a greengrocery shop and show it on the map. Give the street reference and co-ordinates.

______ ______

1. Using bathroom scales, find the **weights** of yourself and three friends. Write in **kilograms** and **grams**.

Name	kg	g

2. Using kitchen scales, find the **weights** of 6 empty containers. Then fill them with water and measure **weights**. Calculate the **net weight** of the water and the **capacity** of each in **millilitres** (ml).

Container	Weight empty	Weight full	Net weight of water	Capacity ml

3. Name things that are weighed on scales like these.

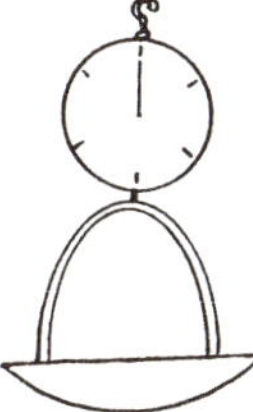

4. Name things that are weighed on scales like these.

5. A family pays rent of **£125** per week for **9** weeks. How much rent altogether? ______

6. The family saved **£155** per week for **9** weeks. How much did they save? ______

7. A baker's shop sold **564** loaves of bread each day for **7** days. How many loaves in total? ______

8. A truck delivered **8** loads of bricks to a building site. Each load contained **890** bricks. How many bricks? ______

9. 7301 x 8 = ______

10. 5348 x 9 = ______

11. 4020 x 6 = ______

12. 9149 x 7 = ______

13. 3466 x 5 = ______

14. 7381 x 4 = ______

15. A girl scored these marks in five tests: 41, 42, 48, 39 and 45. What was her **average** mark? ______

16. Complete the **multiplication** wheel. Check answers with a calculator.

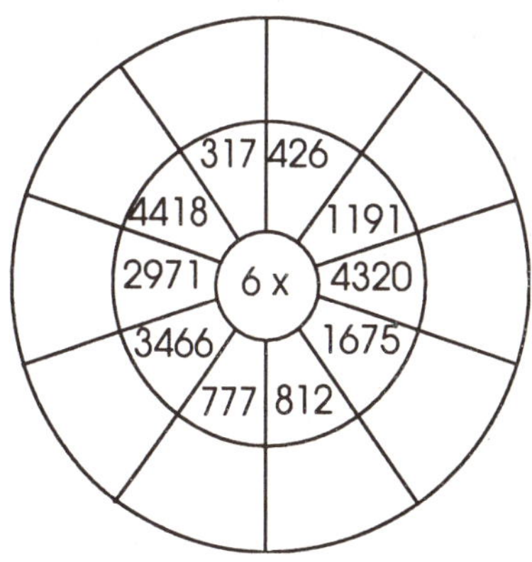

17. You may have heard of the giant who wore **7 league** boots. How far was a **league**? ______

18. How far could the giant walk in one stride? ______

1. 3)983 r ______
2. 5)762 r ______
3. 6)345 r ______
4. 7)619 r ______
5. 4)857 r ______
6. 8)306 r ______
7. 5)831 r ______
8. 6)772 r ______

9. 791 flowerpots are delivered equally to 8 nurseries. How many should each receive? ______

10. How many left over? ______

11. The first nursery refuses to take delivery, so the flowerpots are divided equally among the others. How many more does each receive? ______

12. A rock station has 1782 tracks to play equally over 9 days. How many will be played each day? ______

13. Seven children playing computer games all score the same and their scores total 2 436. What did each score? ______

14. Divide 960 oranges equally into 8 crates. How many **dozen** oranges in each crate? ______

15. Write the sums, then complete.

(a) $664 \div 8 =$ ______

(b) $765 \div 9 =$ ______

(c) $325 \div 5 =$ ______

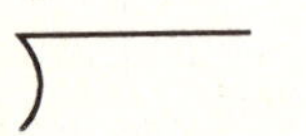

(d) $864 \div 6 =$ ______

16. Read each **temperature** and then write it in numbers and words.

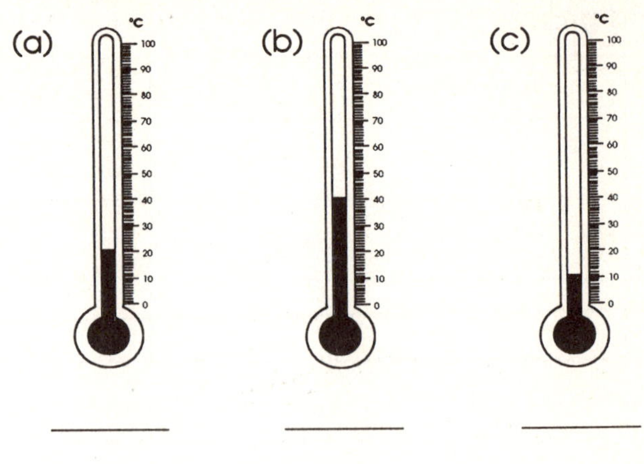

(a) ______ ______
(b) ______ ______
(c) ______ ______

17. Write these **temperatures** in order, lowest to highest .

27°C 14°C 3°C 21°C 33°C 10°C

______

18. Write these **temperatures** in order, highest to lowest.

11°C 24°C 39°C 4°C 18°C 12°C

______

19. Write these **temperatures** in short form.

(a) Freezing point of water ______

(b) Inside a refrigerator ______

(c) Forty-three degrees Celsius ______

(d) Human body temperature ______

(e) Boiling point of water ______

(f) A pleasant, warm room ______

20. In an exercise book, draw a graph of these maximum temperatures for a week in summer.

Sunday	21°C	Thursday	19°C
Monday	14°C	Friday	26°C
Tuesday	17°C	Saturday	16°C
Wednesday	23°C		

1. 10)781 r

2. 10)964 r

3. 10)1735 r

4. 10)1548 r

5. A car factory produces 1 565 cars in 5 days. What is the average number of cars built each day? ______

6. At a chicken farm, 3 550 chickens hatched in 10 days. What is the average number per day? ______

7. A soft drink company offered 2 750 cans of drink equally for 7 sports days. How many more cans needed if there were not to be any left over? ______

8. At the Hotel Posh, **1 323** serviettes are to be placed in the dining room, 9 to a table. How many tables are needed? ______

9. A lottery **syndicate** of 8 people won £2000. How much will each receive? ______

10. What is a **syndicate**? ______

11. Complete the **division** number wheel.

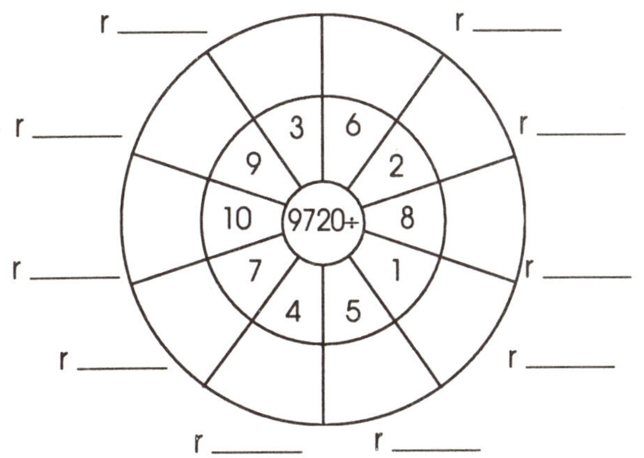

12. Why are most without remainders? ______

13. 6)842 r

14. 7)306 r

15. 8)473 r

16. 9)915 r

17. 7)870 r

18. 5)3601 r

19. 5)2789 r

20. 5)4007 r

21. 10)3716 r

22. 10)4958 r

23. If the **temperature** was 12°C higher than it is now - what would it be? ______

24. Find out what these terms mean.

HYPOTHERMIA: ______

HYPERTHERMIA: ______

25. List three things that would **melt** on a hot day if not kept in a refrigerator.

______

______

______

26. Think of something that is not food, which **melts** on a very hot day.

______

27. Find the **maximum temperatures** for these places yesterday. Look in a newspaper.

Sydney ______ Manchester ______

Glasgow ______ New York ______

Unit 13

This is part of a supermarket receipt.

ALLWAYS SERVES YOU BEST	
	$
BUTTER 250g	0.85
CHEESE 1kg	3.10
T/PASTE 100g	1.93
FOIL	1.34
MUFFINS 15	0.99
DETERGENT 2l	3.68
CORNIES 255g	1.74
SODA WATER 4	1.95
RUBBER GLOVES	1.29
BISCUITS 250g	1.77
Total:	________
Cash:	________
Change:	________

1. Write the total.

2. Write £20 after **Cash**.

3. What change would there be? ________

4. What is the cost of three tubes of toothpaste? ________

5. The supermarket had a sale of 12 bottles of soda water for £6. Is this a better buy than on the receipt? ________

6. The cooking foil was a 10m roll. A 5m roll cost 75 pence. Which was the better buy? ________

7. How much for 60 muffins? ________

8. There is a 10% discount if you buy 4 bottles of detergent. How much would they cost? ________

9. How much for 8 packets of Cornies? ________

10. What would 1kg of butter cost at the price listed? ________

11. On the back of the receipt was a special offer, photo printing £3.95 for a roll of 24. How much for 6 rolls of film? ________

This is a **tally chart** of birds that fed at a bird table one afternoon for one hour.

BIRD TALLIES

Blackbirds	卌 卌 卌 |
Chaffinches	卌 卌 |||
Magpies	卌 ||||
Thrushes	||||
Pigeons	卌 ||
Sparrows	卌 卌 卌 |||
Robins	卌 卌 卌 ||

12. Make up a symbol for a bird and draw it here.

13. In an exercise book draw a picture graph showing the number of birds that came to eat. Use your symbol.

A car dealer made this picture graph to show how many cars he sold in 6 months.

One 🚗 = 10 cars

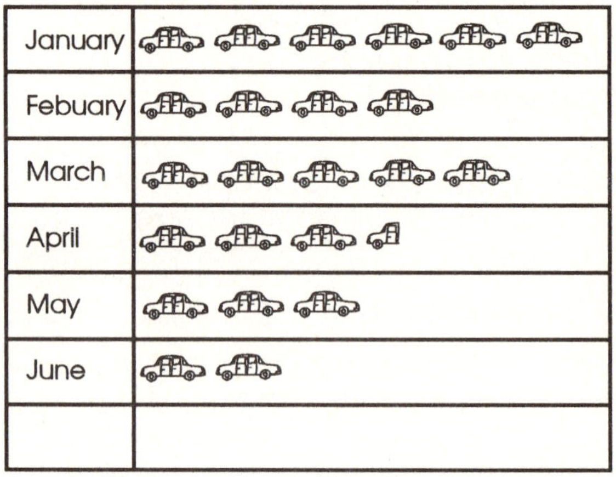

January	🚗 🚗 🚗 🚗 🚗 🚗
Febuary	🚗 🚗 🚗 🚗
March	🚗 🚗 🚗 🚗 🚗
April	🚗 🚗 🚗 ½🚗
May	🚗 🚗 🚗
June	🚗 🚗

14. How many cars were sold in May? ________

15. How many sold in January? ________

16. How many sold in April? ________

17. Give the total number of cars sold between April and June. ________

18. There is a sales pattern trend shown by the graph. What could cause this?

____

19. How many cars sold in the 6 months? ________

20. In July an advertising campaign saw sales reach 55 cars. Show this on the graph.

1. Read the times recorded on these stopwatches. Write them below

(a) 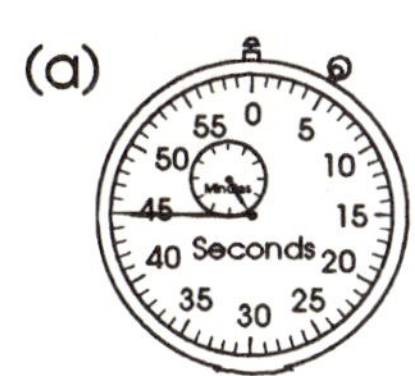
(b) 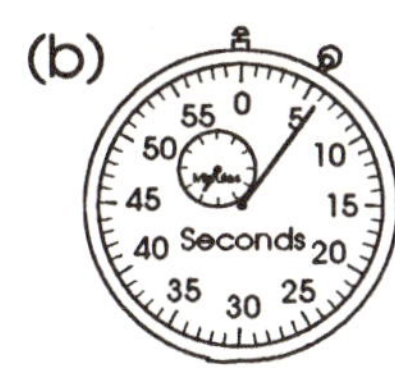
(c) 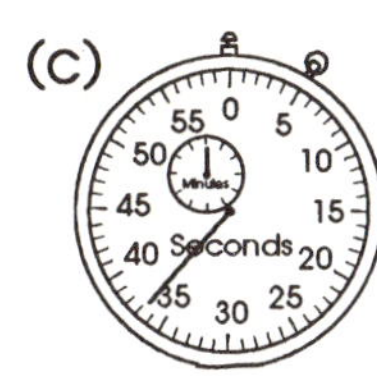

(d) 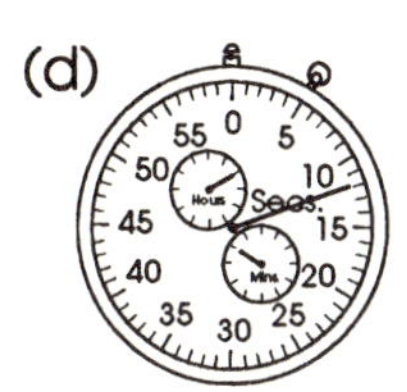
(e) 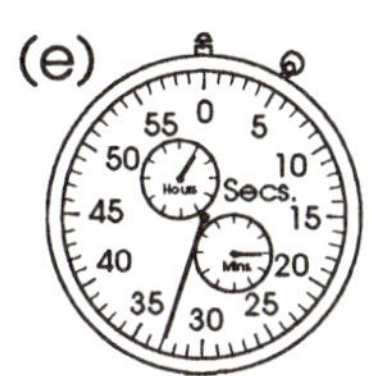
(f) 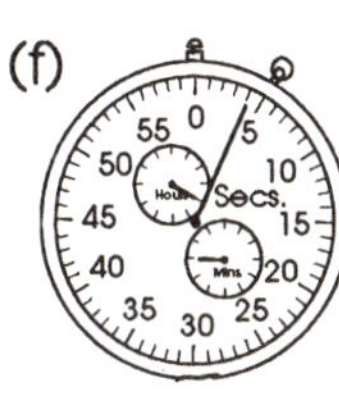

2. Fill in the times on the digital stopwatches.

(a) 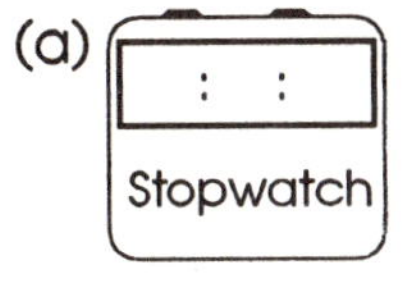

56 seconds

(b) 

6 minutes
32 seconds

(c) 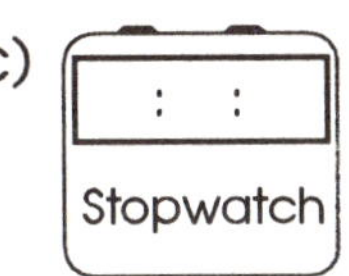

15 minutes
27 seconds
9 hundredths

(d) 

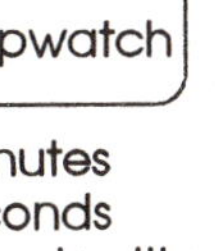

21minutes
8 seconds
72 hundredths

(e) 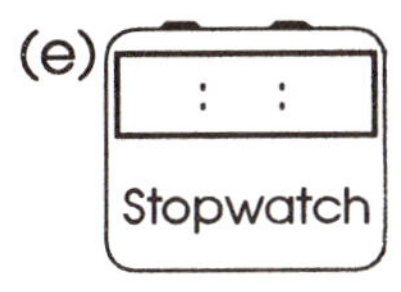

43 minutes
19 seconds
31 hundredths

(f) Stopwatch

6 minutes
43 hundredths

3. How would a stopwatch show these periods of time?

(a) 193 seconds ________

(b) 245 seconds ________

(c) 189 minutes and 78 seconds

____

(d) 75 minutes and 135 seconds

____

4. Apple pies sell for **£1.55** per pie. How much for **6** pies? ________

5. What change from **£10?** ________

6. Rubber gloves sell at **45** pence for a pair, or **£2.35** for **5** pairs. Which is the better buy? ________

7. Brown sugar sells for **£1.32 per kg**, or **66 pence** for **500 g**. Which is the better buy? ________

8. Sliced salami sells for **£1.25 a kilogram.** A whole salami (**1.5kg**) sells for **£1.80**. Which is the better buy? ________

These items are bought at a supermarket.

ALLWAYS SERVES YOU BEST

	£
SULTANAS 1 kg	3.88
RAISINS 1 kg	3.92
BISCUITS 300 g	1.35
RUBBER GLOVES	0.39

9. What is the total cost of these items? ________

10. If there is a 10% discount, how much would they cost? ________

11. Draw hands on these stopwatches.

(a) 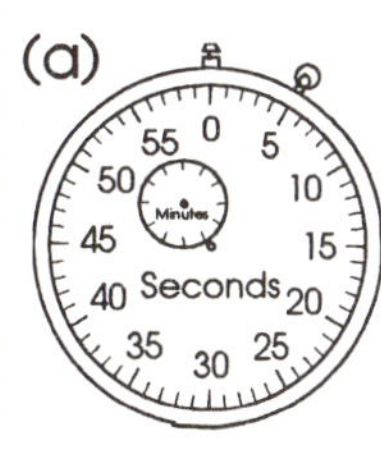

3 minutes
34 seconds

(b) 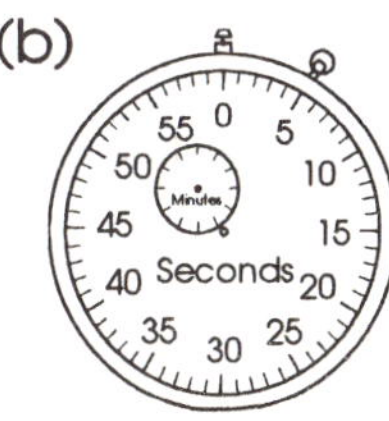

10 minutes
57 seconds

(c) 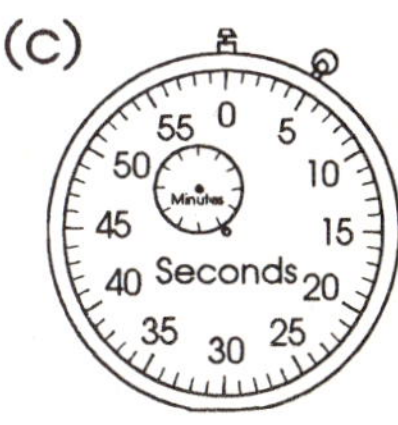

7 minutes
18 seconds

12. How many in half a gross? ________

13. Write these in Roman numerals.

7 ________ 29 ________

13 ________ 82 ________

1. Greta's sister works for £8 per hour. How much will she earn in a 35-hour week? ________

2. Sometimes she works overtime and earns 'time and a half'. What would she earn for seven hours overtime? ________

3. Each week she pays £57.50 tax. How much does she take home? ________

4. A washer-drier cost £960. If I pay £300 deposit and the balance over 6 months, how much do I pay each month? ________

5. List some of your household's weekly expenses.

____

____

____

____

____

6. Do some research and write a few words about each of these.

(a) Credit card ________

____

(b) Charge card ________

____

(c) Cheque ________

____

(d) Cash point ________

____

(e) Bank charges ________

____

A family spends £80 per month at a newsagents. This **bar chart** shows the split.

Newspapers	Magazines	Comics	Sweets

7. What proportion of the whole was spent on newspapers? ________

8. What proportion of the whole was spent on sweets? ________

9. How much was spent on comics? ________

10. How much was spent on magazines? ________

11. How much was spent on newspapers and magazines? ________

This is a **graph** of river heights.

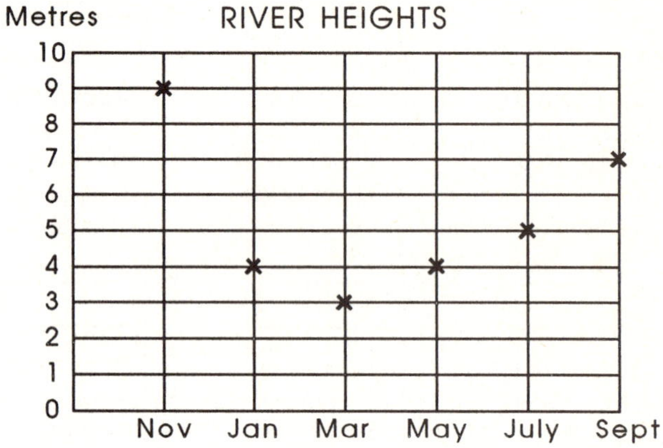

Metres RIVER HEIGHTS

10, 9, 8, 7, 6, 5, 4, 3, 2, 1, 0

Nov Jan Mar May July Sept

12. Join the points to form a **graph**.

13. How high was the river in July? ________

14. What would have been the height in December? ________

15. What would have been the height in August? ________

16. Write down some things that can affect the height of a river.

____

____

____

Write these numbers in words.

1. 2 106 742 ______________________

____

____

2. 9 330 816 ______________________

____

____

3. 98 871 423 ______________________

____

____

Write these words as numbers.

4. Four million seven hundred and sixty- one thousand three hundred and nineteen ______________

5. Eight million twenty-five thousand one hundred and six ______________

6. Sixty-nine million five hundred and eight thousand six hundred and fifty-one ______________

Write these numbers in expanded form.

7. 4 784 603 __________+__________+

______+______+______+______+______

8. 51 359 247 __________+__________+

__________+__________+__________+

______+______+______

9. Write these numbers in falling order.

34 601 879 ______________

31 260 525 ______________

31 620 714 ______________

34 601 789 ______________

31 260 255 ______________

10. What is meant by a **pension**?

____

____

11. What is meant by **life insurance**?

____

____

12. What is meant by **hire purchase**?

____

____

13. What do you do when you **set aside** goods?

____

____

14. A bank offers to pay 6% interest if you invest £1 000 for 12 months.

(a) How much would I earn in 12 months on £1 000? ______

(b) How much would I earn for 18 months on £1 000? ______

(c) How much would I earn on the money in $2\frac{1}{2}$ years? ______

15. The same bank offers short term interest of 8% per annum on £1 000 for 3 months.

(a) How much would I earn in 3 months on £1 000? ______

(b) How much would I earn in 12 months on £1 000? ______

16. Write these words as numbers.

(a) Fourteen million eight hundred and five thousand one hundred and two ______

(b) Ninety-eight million eight hundred thousand and eight______

17. Continue this sequence.

4 3 2 H 5 4 3 G 6 5 4 F 7 ___ ___ ___

Add these sums of money.

1. £4021.75
   3780.33
   + 2194.02

2. £ 457.35
   5692.84
   + 36.95

3. £8761.47
   19.00
   + 366.78

4. £ 23.31
   6389.47
   + 3042.86

5. £7651.07
   8314.37
   + 7651.07

6. £ 586.07
   6175.73
   + 586.07

7. Victoria has a coastline **1 800 km** long; New South Wales' coastline is **1 900 km** and Queensland's is **7 400 km**. How long is the combined coastline of the three Australian states? ______

8. People attended a theme park over three days. *Day 1*: 4 784; *Day 2*: 3 019 and *Day 3*: 3 291. How many attended altogether? ______

9. Mt King is **2 228 m** high, Mt Queen is **1 986 m** and Mt Prince is **1 622 m**. How high are the three together? ______

Check these additions with a calculator. Tick those that are correct or mark with an x if incorrect. If any are wrong, give the correct answer.

10. 3816
    7250
    + 83
    11149

11. 9058
    3168
    + 2863
    15091

12. 7104
    7561
    + 6823
    21488

Draw the **front view**, **side view** and **top view** of these three cube shapes.

13.

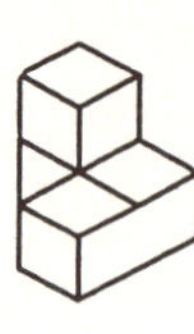

14.

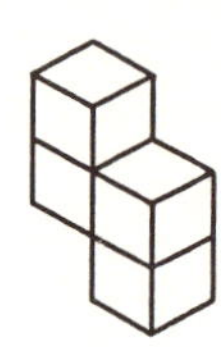

15.

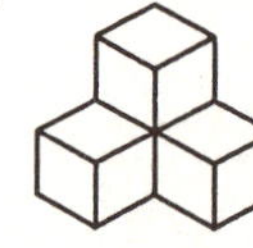

1. Use a stopwatch to find out how long it takes to complete these tasks.

   (a) Put on your shoes ________________

   (b) Drink a glass of water ______________

   (c) Clean your teeth ________________

   (d) Read a page of a book ____________

2. Write the times shown, beneath the digital stopwatches.

   (a) 7:23:19 Stopwatch (b) 1:11:81 Stopwatch (c) 9:48:33 Stopwatch

   ____________ ____________ ____________

   ____________ ____________ ____________

   ____________ ____________ ____________

3. Write a few words about the meaning of these terms.

   (a) Reset ______________________________

   (b) Mode ______________________________

   (c) Delay ______________________________

   (d) Lap ______________________________

   (e) Human error __________________________

   ____

   (f) Jump the gun __________________________

   ____

4.
```
 £7382.75
   206.81
 +3450.26
 ________
```

5.
```
 £ 310.25
    16.71
 +4829.67
 ________
```

6.
```
 £8074.11
   635.04
 +5162.57
 ________
```

7.
```
 £7037.79
    35.21
 +  208.90
 ________
```

8. A rectangular site for a shopping centre is **3 650m** x **2 936m**. What is the perimeter in kilometres? ________

9. These amounts of iron ore were loaded into a ship by conveyor belt: **4 668t**, **5 094t** and **3 875t**. How many tonnes in all? ________

10. The conveyer belt is in three sections: **1 782m**, **2 003m** and **1 890m**. How far did the ore travel in kilometres? ________

11. A bus travels **35km** in half an hour. What is its speed in kilometres per hour? ________

12. On another trip the bus covers **210 km** at **60km/h**. How long did the trip take? ________

13. A reading exercise with a stopwatch shows 265 seconds and six-tenths of a second. How does the digital stopwatch show this?

    [: :] Stopwatch

14. How much will I earn from interest on **$1 500** at **6%** per annum for 12 months? ________

15. What interest do I earn on **£1 200** at an interest rate of **8%** per annum in 6 months? ________

1.
```
  37451
  16023
+ 11489
```

2.
```
  80745
  26319
+ 48713
```

3.
```
  76402
  65137
  49064
+ 83327
```

4.
```
  39024
    196
   7457
+ 63049
```

5.
```
  70184
  34672
  89026
+ 51304
```

6.
```
  41738
      9
   7650
+ 37162
```

7. These were the attendances at a cricket test over five days: 34 927, 71 024, 86 643, 40 173 and 27 589. What was the total attendance for the match? ______

8. If the entry price to the cricket was £8 per head, how much did patrons pay over the five day test? ______

9. An estate agent sold four properties for these amounts: £54 200, £63 750, £71 495 and £148 700. What did his sales total? ______

10. A tropical island had these rainfalls over four years: 2 468mm, 3 519mm, 2 171mm and 1 936mm. What was the total rainfall? ______

11. A newspaper's circulation on Tuesday is 28 756, Wednesday 25 481, 29 846 on Thursday and Friday is 750 less than Thursday. What is the total circulation for the 4 days? ______

12. Fill in the missing numbers.

(a)
```
  _4311
    604
   98_2
+ 50436
 14518_
```

(b)
```
  9_648
     _6
  76_04
+  897_
 _76218
```

13. Use cubes to make these shapes, then draw them on the grid.

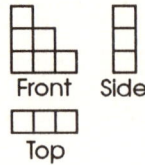

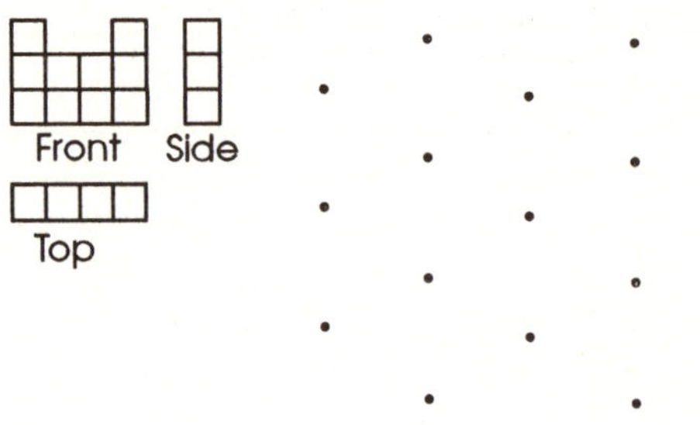

14. Draw the **front view** and **top view** of this **3-D** shape after **doubling** the height and the length.

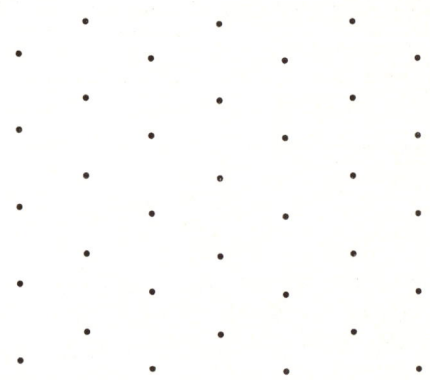

1. Calculate the **areas** of these rectangles. Use **1cm squared grid paper** if you need help.

	Length (cm)	Width (cm)	Area (cm^2)
(a)	3	2	
(b)	2	4	
(c)	5	2	
(d)	7	4	
(e)	3	6	
(f)	8	3	

2. Write down the **length** and **width** of these rectangles in **centimetres** and calculate the area.

	Length		Width		Area
(a) One side of a ruler	______	x	______	=	______
(b) The front cover of a dictionary	______	x	______	=	______
(c) One face of a brick	______	x	______	=	______
(d) The base of a calculator	______	x	______	=	______
(e) A quarter page advertisement in a newspaper	______	x	______	=	______

3. A car showroom has an area of **5 000m²**. The frontage is **50m.** What is the length of the showroom? ______

4. A sheet of plywood is **3m x 4m.** A builder cuts two pieces **6m²** and **4m².** How many square metres left? ______

5. A city block of land has an area of **6 000m².** A parking space of **30m x 20m** has to be set aside. How much land is left for an office block? ______

6. A swimming pool is 9m x 5m. What is the **surface area** of the water? ______

7. There is a pathway 2m wide around the pool, and then a fence. What is the total area fenced in? ______

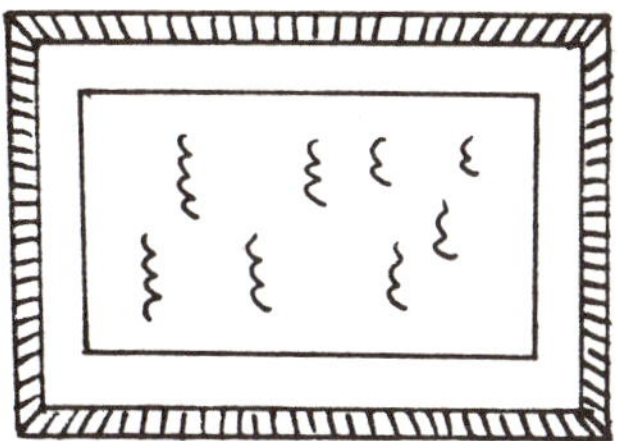

8. What is the **area** of path? ______

9. What is the **perimeter** of the area fenced in? ______

10. The fence is 2m high and made of wood. What **area** of wood is needed? ______

11. When the pool is full it holds **78 000l** of water. How many litres when half full? ______

12. Water can be pumped out of the pool at **50l per minute.** How much in one hour? ______

13. At that rate, how long would it take to empty the pool? ______

14.
```
  73681
  20495
+ 19387
_______
```

15.
```
  40937
  15405
+ 97862
_______
```

16.
```
  738407
  116590
+ 360242
________
```

17.
```
  579714
  326175
  816753
+   2636
________
```

18.
```
  831642
     119
   63854
+ 114731
________
```

19.
```
     684
  713245
   91763
+ 127598
________
```

Unit 17

1.
```
  8000
- 7000
```

2.
```
  6000
- 3000
```

3.
```
  7600
- 5000
```

4.
```
  5431
- 4000
```

5.
```
  6148
- 6000
```

6.
```
  8615
- 2000
```

7.
```
  9364
- 7153
```

8.
```
  8569
- 4537
```

9.
```
  4093
- 2404
```

10. The first coach service between Shelborne and Melchester began in 1853. In 1887 the cities were linked by rail. How many years between these events? ______

11. The first recorded Olympic Games were held in 776 B.C. and they were banned in A.D. 393. How many years between these dates? ______

12. The modern Olympic Games began in 1896. How many years between the banning and the new beginning? ______

13. The River Nile is 6 670km long. The Thames is 388km long. How much longer is the Nile? ______

14. Mt McKinley (6 194m) is the highest mountain in North America. Mt Kosciusko (Australia) is 2 280m. What is the difference in metres? ______

15. Francis Drake set out on the voyage that would take him around the world in 1577. How many years ago was this? ______

Make card copies of these shapes. Place the copy over the printed outline, insert a pin in the centre, then **rotate** through **360°.** Count and record the number of times the cut-out matches the shape. If it doesn't match record 0.

16.

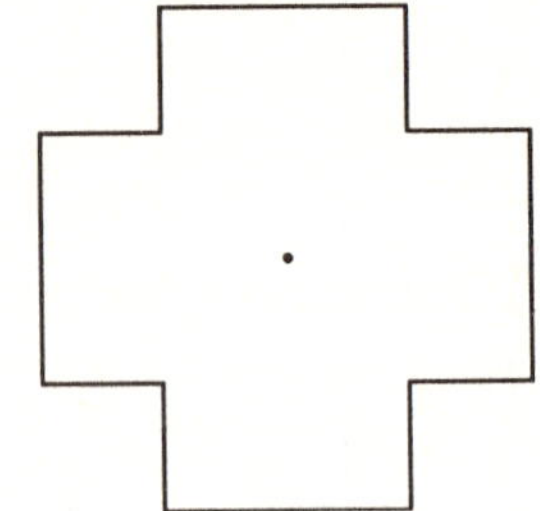

______

17.

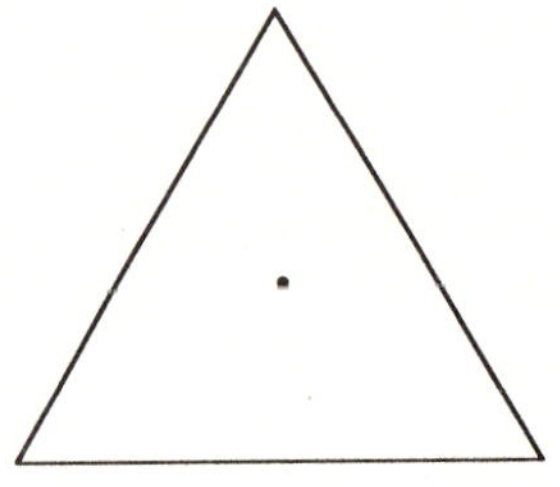

______

18.

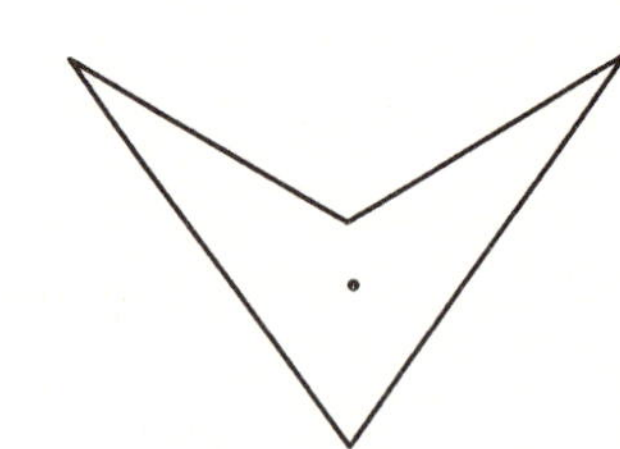

______

19.

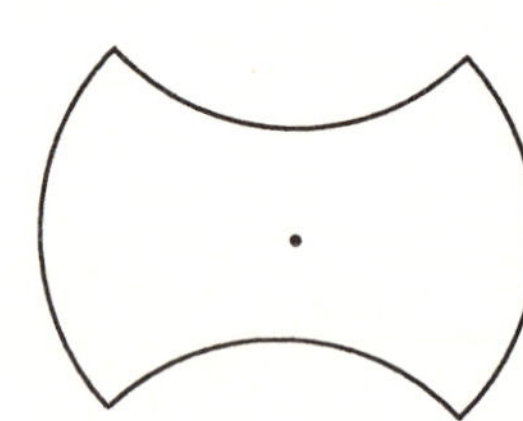

______

20.

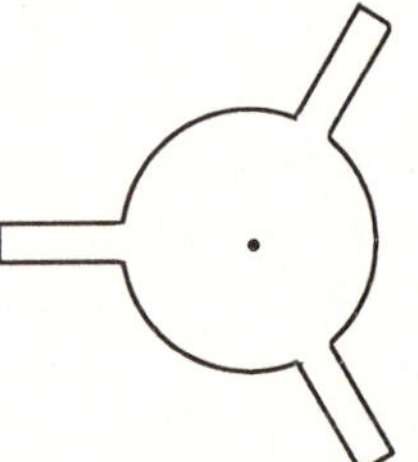

______

1. Draw a **cube** 1m x 1m x 1m, using a scale 2cm = 1m. This is a **cubic metre.**

2. Draw a **rectangular prism,** using the same scale with sides 0.5m x 2m x 1m. It is also a **cubic metre** in volume.

3. Estimate the capacity in $\mathbf{m^3}$ of the following.

(a) A public telephone box ________

(b) A wardrobe ________

(c) A washing machine ________

(d) A shop's drink cabinet ________

(e) A bath ________

(f) A storage cupboard ________

4. What is the capacity of a container that measures 2m x 3m x 4m? ________

5. List containers, less than **one cubic metre,** that have capacity measured as $\mathbf{m^3}$, e.g. $0.5m^3$.

____

____

____

____

6.	7.	8.
6310	7406	9016
- 5208	-3195	-9006
______	______	______

9.	10.	11.
3131	8741	6383
-1313	-7852	-3863
______	______	______

12. **7 802** apples are picked in an orchard and **5 904** are packed in cartons by the end of the day. How many not packed? ________

13. Of those left, **496** are found to be bad. How many good ones?________

14. Lee had **2 076** coins in his collection. **163** were American, **239** were British. How many from other countries? ________

15. Yvette collected French stamps, but when she counted her collection she found only **1 084** out of **3 481** were French. How many were not French?________

16. Those that were not French she sold for 5 pence each. How much did she receive? ________

17. Find out the capacity of a family car in $\mathbf{m^3}$. ________

18. A girl scored 83, 28, 35 and 54 in four games of cards. What was her average score? ________

19. Write these in Roman numerals.

(a) 39 ____________ (b) 58 ____________

(c) 140 ____________ (d) 505 ____________

1. 3644
 -2557
 ______

2. 9048
 -8759
 ______

3. 8899
 -6905
 ______

4. 6001
 -5112
 ______

5. 5347
 -2458
 ______

6. 4756
 -3819
 ______

7. A sprinkler system is set to come on at **1630 hours** and shut off at **2045 hours.** How many minutes will it run? ______

8. A car is advertised at **£6 995.** Another dealer offers a similar car for **£5 870.** How much cheaper is the second car? ______

9. A woman earns **£3 475** in a year. **£2 864** goes in rent, taxes, food and other expenses. How much does she have left? ______

10. It is **1 439km** from Broome to Townsville and **1 720km** to Chinley further north. How far between Townsville and Chinley? ______

11. What is the difference in population between Melville (34 450) and Lexton (5 502)? ______

12. 67__0
 -5631
 1109

13. 564__
 -__538
 1111

14. 9__37
 -7348
 20__9

15. £199.__2
 -1__4.71
 £ 1__.91

16. £__89.87
 -8__8.92
 £ 9__.95

17. Without making cut-outs, colour the shapes that will **rotate symmetrically.**

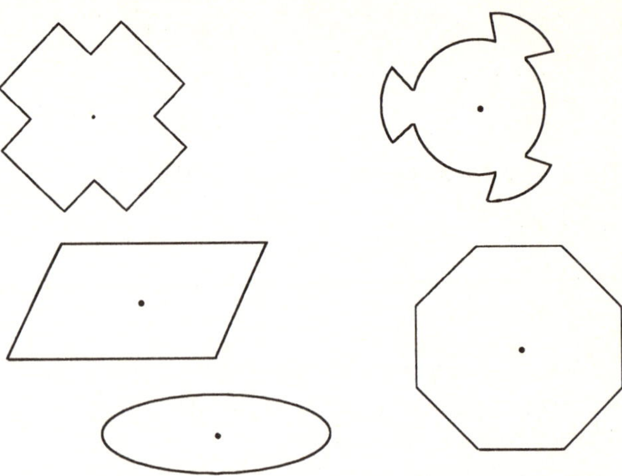

18. Draw three different shapes that will **rotate symmetrically.** State the number of times each will match when rotated through **360°.**

(a) ______

(b) ______

(c) ______

1. Complete this table:
   (a) 1 cubic centimetre has a capacity of ________ millilitres
   (b) 1 millilitre of water has a weight equal to ________ gram
   (c) 1 litre of water = ________ millilitres
   (d) 1 litre of water has a weight of ________ kilogram

2. Complete this table.
   (a) 400ml of water has a weight of ______g
   (b) 750ml of water has a weight of ______g
   (c) 1 500ml of water has a weight of ______kg

3. What is the **weight** of 2l of water?________

4. Use a measuring jug of water to find the **displacement volume** of these objects.

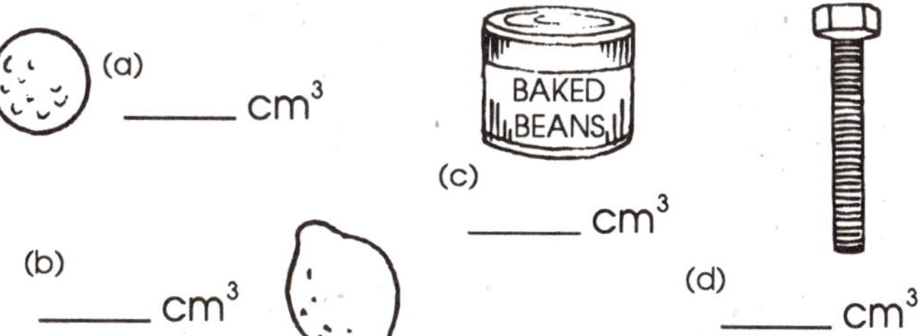

(a) ______ cm^3

(b) ______ cm^3

(c) ______ cm^3

(d) ______ cm^3

5. Find and record the **weight** of each object above. *(Don't forget g.)*

golf ball__________ bolt __________

lemon __________ can__________

6. Write a short report about the link between **volumes** and **weights** .

____

____

____

7. How many litres in one **cubic metre?** ________

8. How many litres are needed to fill a tank **35m³** tank? ________

9. What is the **weight** of 5l of water? ________

10. What is the weight of 3.75l of water? ________

11. 7 500ml = ________l

12. 4 750ml of water has a weight of ________kg

13. How many times will this shape match when rotated through **360°?** ________

14. How many times will this shape match when rotated through **360°?** ________

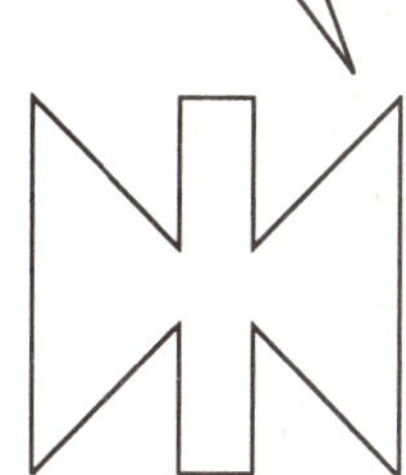

15.	16.	17.
6537	8307	6408
- 2468	-7415	-4680

18.	19.	20.
9879	8963	1053
-3248	-1979	-1049

21. Complete this sum, then make up a subtraction story.

4 550 - 3 440 = ________

____

____

____

22. A motor spare parts shop had **8 320** indicator bulbs at the annual stock take. Since then it has sold **4 725** bulbs. How many bulbs in stock? ________

23. A man had **£5 690** in the bank. He put in a cheque for **£110** and took out **£440** in cash. How much left in the bank?________

Unit 19

1. 10 x 93 = ______
2. 10 x 70 = ______
3. 11 x 49 = ______
4. 11 x 84 = ______
5. 12 x 37 = ______
6. 12 x 53 = ______
7. 13 x 78 = ______
8. 14 x 91 = ______
9. 15 x 67 = ______
10. 16 x 45 = ______

11. Match each **sum** to the correct answer, and then check with a calculator.

48 x 25	**1 224**	72 x 17
	1 428	
65 x 22	**1 444**	57 x 24
	1 512	
45 x 35	**1 200**	38 x 38
	1 368	
68 x 21	**1 430**	42 x 36
	1 575	

Estimate these **answers**, then find the exact answer.

12. 28 x 26 ______ Estimate

13. 33 x 19 ______ Estimate

14. 46 x 25 ______ Estimate

15. 69 x 24 ______ Estimate

16. 77 x 33 ______ Estimate

Find the **weight** of each item using suitable **scales.** Record results in both **grams** and **kilograms.** Tick the more appropriate measure.

17. Yourself ______g ☐ ______kg ☐

18. A packed suitcase ______g ☐ ______kg ☐

19. A bag of oranges ______g ☐ ______kg ☐

20. A dog or a cat ______g ☐ ______kg ☐

21. A melon ______g ☐ ______kg ☐

22. A packet of pencils ______g ☐ ______kg ☐

23. List the scales and weighing machines in your home.

______

______

24. List four shops in a shopping centre where scales are used.

______

______

______

______

25. Find the **weight** of an unopened can of drink, and the **weight** of an empty can. Then calculate the **net weight** of the contents.

Gross Weight ______ Empty Can ______ Net Contents ______

26. Do the same for a jar of honey.

Gross Weight ______ Empty Jar ______ Net Contents ______

LEAP AHEAD

with

MATHS

Answers
Book 7

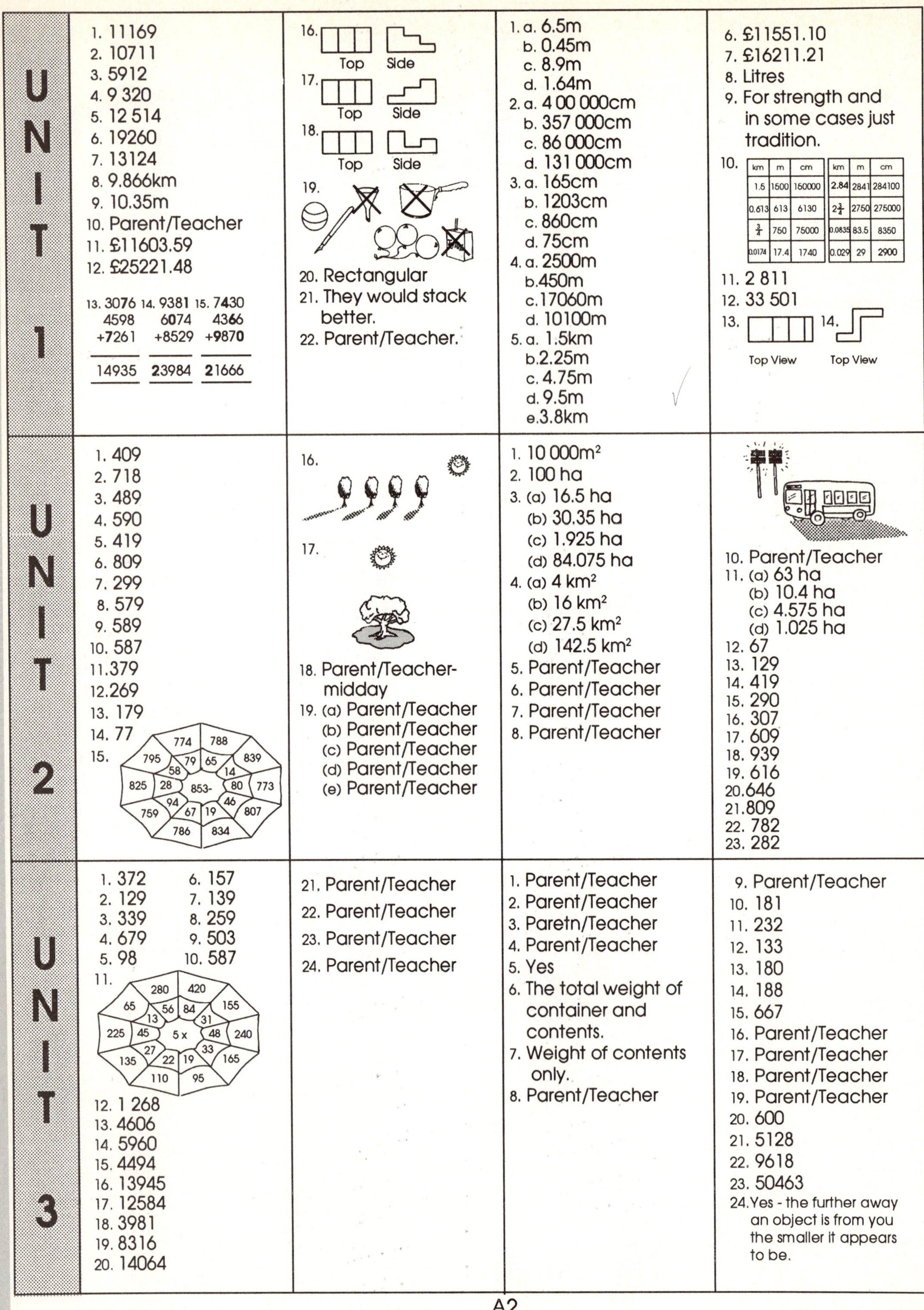

UNIT 1

1. 11169
2. 10711
3. 5912
4. 9 320
5. 12 514
6. 19260
7. 13124
8. 9.866km
9. 10.35m
10. Parent/Teacher
11. £11603.59
12. £25221.48

13. 3076	14. 9381	15. 7430
4598	6074	4366
+7261	+8529	+9870
14935	23984	21666

16. Top Side
17. Top Side
18. Top Side
19.
20. Rectangular
21. They would stack better.
22. Parent/Teacher.

1. a. 6.5m
   b. 0.45m
   c. 8.9m
   d. 1.64m
2. a. 4 00 000cm
   b. 357 000cm
   c. 86 000cm
   d. 131 000cm
3. a. 165cm
   b. 1203cm
   c. 860cm
   d. 75cm
4. a. 2500m
   b.450m
   c.17060m
   d. 10100m
5. a. 1.5km
   b.2.25m
   c. 4.75m
   d. 9.5m
   e.3.8km

6. £11551.10
7. £16211.21
8. Litres
9. For strength and in some cases just tradition.
10.

km	m	cm
1.5	1500	150000
0.613	613	6130
$\frac{3}{4}$	750	75000
0.0174	17.4	1740

km	m	cm
2.84	2841	284100
$2\frac{3}{4}$	2750	275000
0.0835	83.5	8350
0.029	29	2900

11. 2 811
12. 33 501
13. Top View
14. Top View

UNIT 2

1. 409
2. 718
3. 489
4. 590
5. 419
6. 809
7. 299
8. 579
9. 589
10. 587
11. 379
12. 269
13. 179
14. 77
15.

16.
17.
18. Parent/Teacher- midday
19. (a) Parent/Teacher
    (b) Parent/Teacher
    (c) Parent/Teacher
    (d) Parent/Teacher
    (e) Parent/Teacher

1. 10 000m²
2. 100 ha
3. (a) 16.5 ha
   (b) 30.35 ha
   (c) 1.925 ha
   (d) 84.075 ha
4. (a) 4 km²
   (b) 16 km²
   (c) 27.5 km²
   (d) 142.5 km²
5. Parent/Teacher
6. Parent/Teacher
7. Parent/Teacher
8. Parent/Teacher

10. Parent/Teacher
11. (a) 63 ha
    (b) 10.4 ha
    (c) 4.575 ha
    (d) 1.025 ha
12. 67
13. 129
14. 419
15. 290
16. 307
17. 609
18. 939
19. 616
20. 646
21. 809
22. 782
23. 282

UNIT 3

1. 372
2. 129
3. 339
4. 679
5. 98
6. 157
7. 139
8. 259
9. 503
10. 587
11.

12. 1 268
13. 4606
14. 5960
15. 4494
16. 13945
17. 12584
18. 3981
19. 8316
20. 14064

21. Parent/Teacher
22. Parent/Teacher
23. Parent/Teacher
24. Parent/Teacher

1. Parent/Teacher
2. Parent/Teacher
3. Paretn/Teacher
4. Parent/Teacher
5. Yes
6. The total weight of container and contents.
7. Weight of contents only.
8. Parent/Teacher

9. Parent/Teacher
10. 181
11. 232
12. 133
13. 180
14. 188
15. 667
16. Parent/Teacher
17. Parent/Teacher
18. Parent/Teacher
19. Parent/Teacher
20. 600
21. 5128
22. 9618
23. 50463
24. Yes - the further away an object is from you the smaller it appears to be.

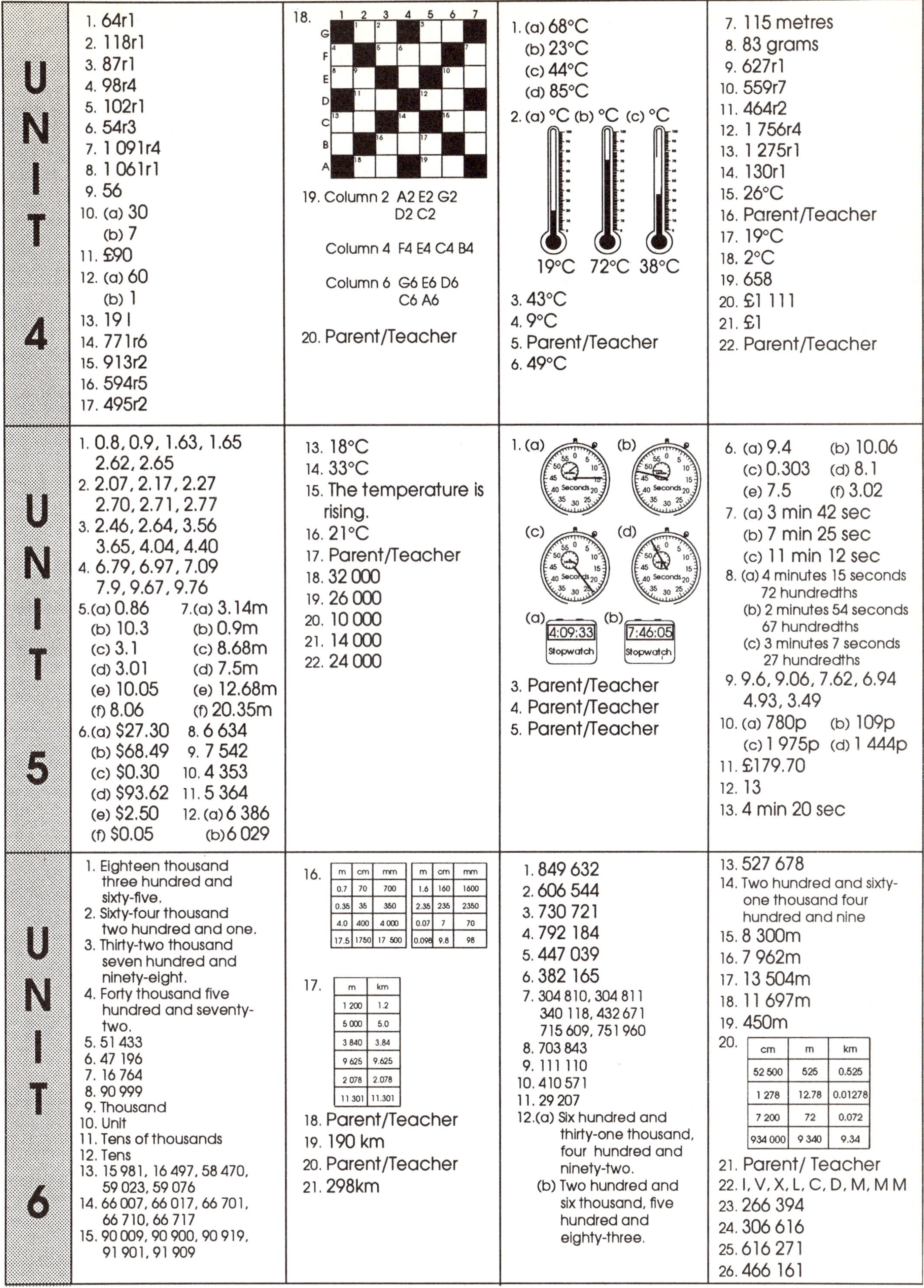

UNIT 4

1. 64r1
2. 118r1
3. 87r1
4. 98r4
5. 102r1
6. 54r3
7. 1 091r4
8. 1 061r1
9. 56
10. (a) 30
    (b) 7
11. £90
12. (a) 60
    (b) 1
13. 19 I
14. 771r6
15. 913r2
16. 594r5
17. 495r2

18.

19. Column 2 A2 E2 G2 D2 C2

    Column 4 F4 E4 C4 B4

    Column 6 G6 E6 D6 C6 A6

20. Parent/Teacher

1. (a) 68°C
   (b) 23°C
   (c) 44°C
   (d) 85°C
2. (a) °C (b) °C (c) °C

   19°C 72°C 38°C
3. 43°C
4. 9°C
5. Parent/Teacher
6. 49°C

7. 115 metres
8. 83 grams
9. 627r1
10. 559r7
11. 464r2
12. 1 756r4
13. 1 275r1
14. 130r1
15. 26°C
16. Parent/Teacher
17. 19°C
18. 2°C
19. 658
20. £1 111
21. £1
22. Parent/Teacher

UNIT 5

1. 0.8, 0.9, 1.63, 1.65
   2.62, 2.65
2. 2.07, 2.17, 2.27
   2.70, 2.71, 2.77
3. 2.46, 2.64, 3.56
   3.65, 4.04, 4.40
4. 6.79, 6.97, 7.09
   7.9, 9.67, 9.76
5. (a) 0.86
   (b) 10.3
   (c) 3.1
   (d) 3.01
   (e) 10.05
   (f) 8.06
6. (a) $27.30
   (b) $68.49
   (c) $0.30
   (d) $93.62
   (e) $2.50
   (f) $0.05
7. (a) 3.14m
   (b) 0.9m
   (c) 8.68m
   (d) 7.5m
   (e) 12.68m
   (f) 20.35m
8. 6 634
9. 7 542
10. 4 353
11. 5 364
12. (a) 6 386
    (b) 6 029

13. 18°C
14. 33°C
15. The temperature is rising.
16. 21°C
17. Parent/Teacher
18. 32 000
19. 26 000
20. 10 000
21. 14 000
22. 24 000

1. (a) (b) (c) (d)

2. (a) 4:09:33 Stopwatch (b) 7:46:05 Stopwatch
3. Parent/Teacher
4. Parent/Teacher
5. Parent/Teacher

6. (a) 9.4 (b) 10.06
   (c) 0.303 (d) 8.1
   (e) 7.5 (f) 3.02
7. (a) 3 min 42 sec
   (b) 7 min 25 sec
   (c) 11 min 12 sec
8. (a) 4 minutes 15 seconds 72 hundredths
   (b) 2 minutes 54 seconds 67 hundredths
   (c) 3 minutes 7 seconds 27 hundredths
9. 9.6, 9.06, 7.62, 6.94
   4.93, 3.49
10. (a) 780p (b) 109p
    (c) 1 975p (d) 1 444p
11. £179.70
12. 13
13. 4 min 20 sec

UNIT 6

1. Eighteen thousand three hundred and sixty-five.
2. Sixty-four thousand two hundred and one.
3. Thirty-two thousand seven hundred and ninety-eight.
4. Forty thousand five hundred and seventy-two.
5. 51 433
6. 47 196
7. 16 764
8. 90 999
9. Thousand
10. Unit
11. Tens of thousands
12. Tens
13. 15 981, 16 497, 58 470, 59 023, 59 076
14. 66 007, 66 017, 66 701, 66 710, 66 717
15. 90 009, 90 900, 90 919, 91 901, 91 909

16.

m	cm	mm
0.7	70	700
0.35	35	350
4.0	400	4 000
17.5	1750	17 500

m	cm	mm
1.6	160	1600
2.35	235	2350
0.07	7	70
0.098	9.8	98

17.

m	km
1 200	1.2
5 000	5.0
3 840	3.84
9 625	9.625
2 078	2.078
11 301	11.301

18. Parent/Teacher
19. 190 km
20. Parent/Teacher
21. 298km

1. 849 632
2. 606 544
3. 730 721
4. 792 184
5. 447 039
6. 382 165
7. 304 810, 304 811
   340 118, 432 671
   715 609, 751 960
8. 703 843
9. 111 110
10. 410 571
11. 29 207
12. (a) Six hundred and thirty-one thousand, four hundred and ninety-two.
    (b) Two hundred and six thousand, five hundred and eighty-three.

13. 527 678
14. Two hundred and sixty-one thousand four hundred and nine
15. 8 300m
16. 7 962m
17. 13 504m
18. 11 697m
19. 450m
20.

cm	m	km
52 500	525	0.525
1 278	12.78	0.01278
7 200	72	0.072
934 000	9 340	9.34

21. Parent/ Teacher
22. I, V, X, L, C, D, M, M M
23. 266 394
24. 306 616
25. 616 271
26. 466 161

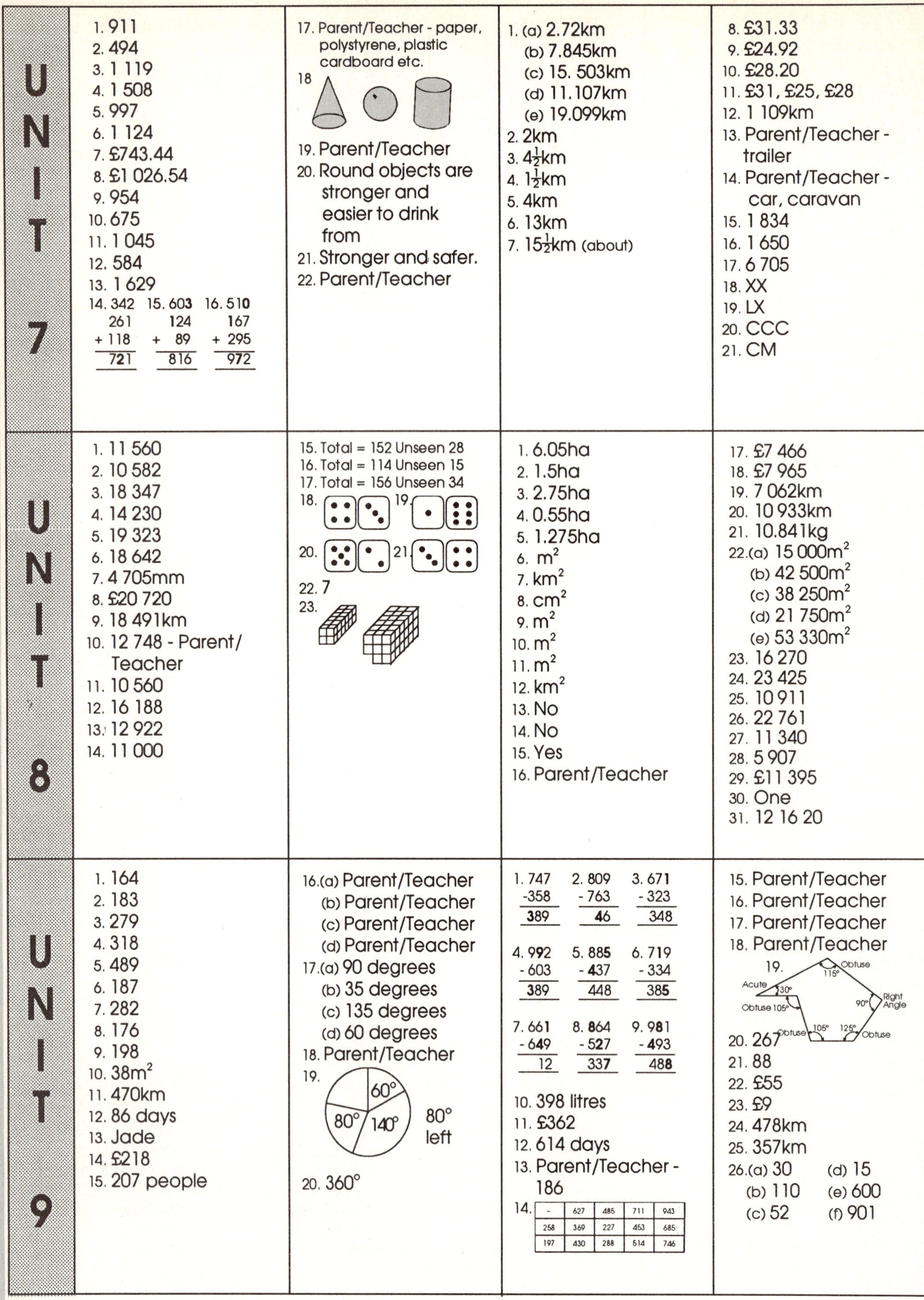

UNIT 7

1. 911
2. 494
3. 1 119
4. 1 508
5. 997
6. 1 124
7. £743.44
8. £1 026.54
9. 954
10. 675
11. 1 045
12. 584
13. 1 629

14. 342 + 261 + 118 = 721
15. 603 + 124 + 89 = 816
16. 510 + 167 + 295 = 972

17. Parent/Teacher - paper, polystyrene, plastic cardboard etc.
18.
19. Parent/Teacher
20. Round objects are stronger and easier to drink from
21. Stronger and safer.
22. Parent/Teacher

1. (a) 2.72km
   (b) 7.845km
   (c) 15. 503km
   (d) 11.107km
   (e) 19.099km
2. 2km
3. $4\frac{1}{2}$km
4. $1\frac{1}{2}$km
5. 4km
6. 13km
7. $15\frac{1}{2}$km (about)

8. £31.33
9. £24.92
10. £28.20
11. £31, £25, £28
12. 1 109km
13. Parent/Teacher - trailer
14. Parent/Teacher - car, caravan
15. 1 834
16. 1 650
17. 6 705
18. XX
19. LX
20. CCC
21. CM

UNIT 8

1. 11 560
2. 10 582
3. 18 347
4. 14 230
5. 19 323
6. 18 642
7. 4 705mm
8. £20 720
9. 18 491km
10. 12 748 - Parent/Teacher
11. 10 560
12. 16 188
13. 12 922
14. 11 000

15. Total = 152 Unseen 28
16. Total = 114 Unseen 15
17. Total = 156 Unseen 34
18.
19.
20.
21.
22. 7
23.

1. 6.05ha
2. 1.5ha
3. 2.75ha
4. 0.55ha
5. 1.275ha
6. m^2
7. km^2
8. cm^2
9. m^2
10. m^2
11. m^2
12. km^2
13. No
14. No
15. Yes
16. Parent/Teacher

17. £7 466
18. £7 965
19. 7 062km
20. 10 933km
21. 10.841kg
22. (a) 15 000m^2
    (b) 42 500m^2
    (c) 38 250m^2
    (d) 21 750m^2
    (e) 53 330m^2
23. 16 270
24. 23 425
25. 10 911
26. 22 761
27. 11 340
28. 5 907
29. £11 395
30. One
31. 12 16 20

UNIT 9

1. 164
2. 183
3. 279
4. 318
5. 489
6. 187
7. 282
8. 176
9. 198
10. 38m^2
11. 470km
12. 86 days
13. Jade
14. £218
15. 207 people

16. (a) Parent/Teacher
    (b) Parent/Teacher
    (c) Parent/Teacher
    (d) Parent/Teacher
17. (a) 90 degrees
    (b) 35 degrees
    (c) 135 degrees
    (d) 60 degrees
18. Parent/Teacher
19.

80° left
20. 360°

1. 747 - 358 = 389
2. 809 - 763 = 46
3. 671 - 323 = 348
4. 992 - 603 = 389
5. 885 - 437 = 448
6. 719 - 334 = 385
7. 661 - 649 = 12
8. 864 - 527 = 337
9. 981 - 493 = 488
10. 398 litres
11. £362
12. 614 days
13. Parent/Teacher - 186
14.

-	627	485	711	943
258	369	227	453	685
197	430	288	514	746

15. Parent/Teacher
16. Parent/Teacher
17. Parent/Teacher
18. Parent/Teacher
19.

20. 267
21. 88
22. £55
23. £9
24. 478km
25. 357km
26. (a) 30 (d) 15
    (b) 110 (e) 600
    (c) 52 (f) 901

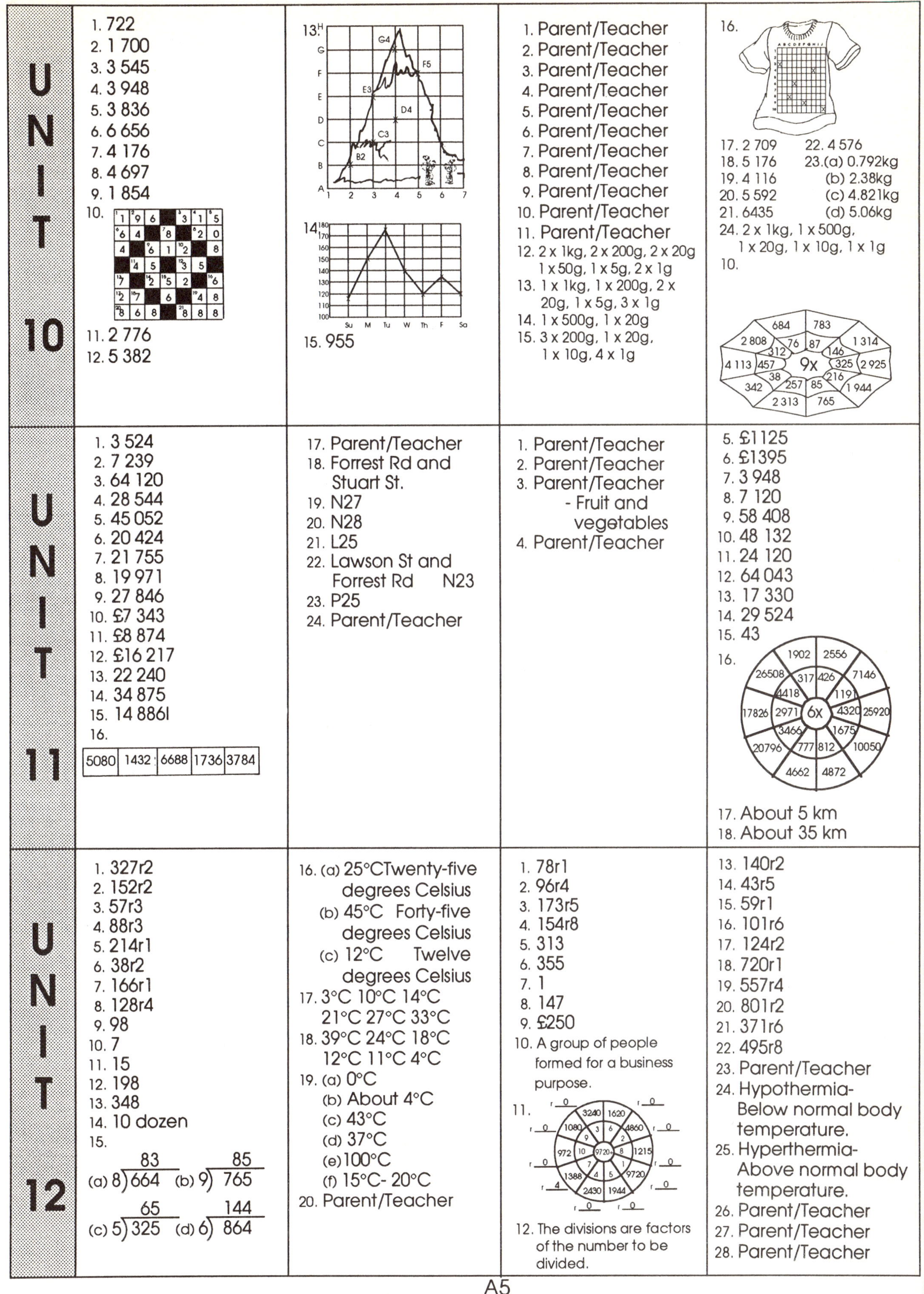

UNIT 10

1. 722
2. 1 700
3. 3 545
4. 3 948
5. 3 836
6. 6 656
7. 4 176
8. 4 697
9. 1 854
10.

1	9	6	■	3	1	5
6	4	■	8	■	2	0
4	■	6	1	2	■	8
■	4	5	■	3	5	■
7	■	2	5	2	■	6
2	7	■	6	■	4	8
8	6	8	■	8	8	8

11. 2 776
12. 5 382

13.

14.

15. 955

1. Parent/Teacher
2. Parent/Teacher
3. Parent/Teacher
4. Parent/Teacher
5. Parent/Teacher
6. Parent/Teacher
7. Parent/Teacher
8. Parent/Teacher
9. Parent/Teacher
10. Parent/Teacher
11. Parent/Teacher
12. 2 x 1kg, 2 x 200g, 2 x 20g 1 x 50g, 1 x 5g, 2 x 1g
13. 1 x 1kg, 1 x 200g, 2 x 20g, 1 x 5g, 3 x 1g
14. 1 x 500g, 1 x 20g
15. 3 x 200g, 1 x 20g, 1 x 10g, 4 x 1g

16.

17. 2 709
18. 5 176
19. 4 116
20. 5 592
21. 6435
22. 4 576
23. (a) 0.792kg
(b) 2.38kg
(c) 4.821kg
(d) 5.06kg
24. 2 x 1kg, 1 x 500g, 1 x 20g, 1 x 10g, 1 x 1g

10.

UNIT 11

1. 3 524
2. 7 239
3. 64 120
4. 28 544
5. 45 052
6. 20 424
7. 21 755
8. 19 971
9. 27 846
10. £7 343
11. £8 874
12. £16 217
13. 22 240
14. 34 875
15. 14 886l
16.

5080	1432	6688	1736	3784

17. Parent/Teacher
18. Forrest Rd and Stuart St.
19. N27
20. N28
21. L25
22. Lawson St and Forrest Rd N23
23. P25
24. Parent/Teacher

1. Parent/Teacher
2. Parent/Teacher
3. Parent/Teacher - Fruit and vegetables
4. Parent/Teacher

5. £1125
6. £1395
7. 3 948
8. 7 120
9. 58 408
10. 48 132
11. 24 120
12. 64 043
13. 17 330
14. 29 524
15. 43
16.

17. About 5 km
18. About 35 km

UNIT 12

1. 327r2
2. 152r2
3. 57r3
4. 88r3
5. 214r1
6. 38r2
7. 166r1
8. 128r4
9. 98
10. 7
11. 15
12. 198
13. 348
14. 10 dozen
15.

(a) $8\overline{)664}$ = 83 (b) $9\overline{)765}$ = 85

(c) $5\overline{)325}$ = 65 (d) $6\overline{)864}$ = 144

16. (a) 25°C Twenty-five degrees Celsius
(b) 45°C Forty-five degrees Celsius
(c) 12°C Twelve degrees Celsius
17. 3°C 10°C 14°C 21°C 27°C 33°C
18. 39°C 24°C 18°C 12°C 11°C 4°C
19. (a) 0°C
(b) About 4°C
(c) 43°C
(d) 37°C
(e) 100°C
(f) 15°C- 20°C
20. Parent/Teacher

1. 78r1
2. 96r4
3. 173r5
4. 154r8
5. 313
6. 355
7. 1
8. 147
9. £250
10. A group of people formed for a business purpose.
11.

12. The divisions are factors of the number to be divided.

13. 140r2
14. 43r5
15. 59r1
16. 101r6
17. 124r2
18. 720r1
19. 557r4
20. 801r2
21. 371r6
22. 495r8
23. Parent/Teacher
24. Hypothermia- Below normal body temperature.
25. Hyperthermia- Above normal body temperature.
26. Parent/Teacher
27. Parent/Teacher
28. Parent/Teacher

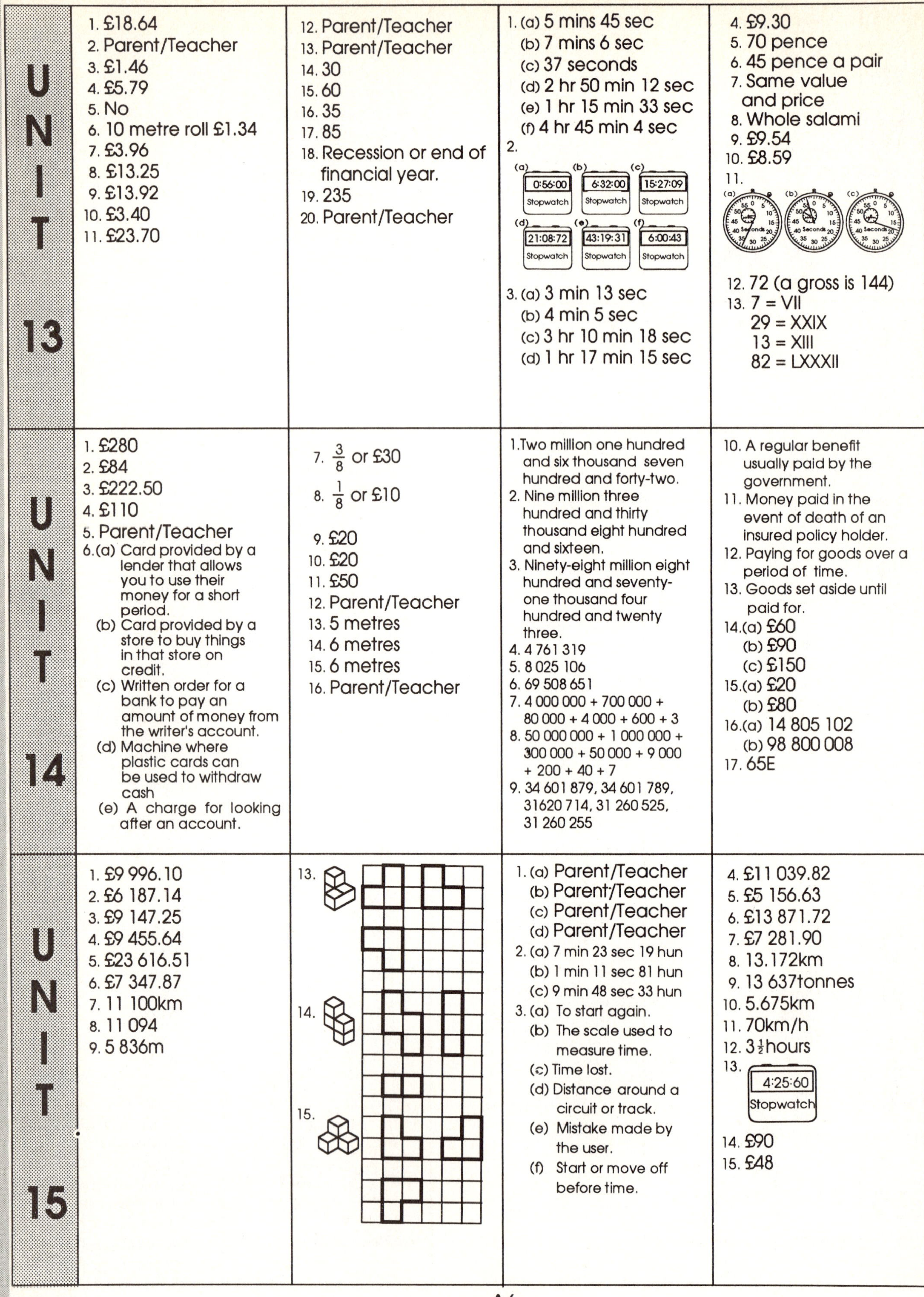

UNIT 13

1. £18.64
2. Parent/Teacher
3. £1.46
4. £5.79
5. No
6. 10 metre roll £1.34
7. £3.96
8. £13.25
9. £13.92
10. £3.40
11. £23.70
12. Parent/Teacher
13. Parent/Teacher
14. 30
15. 60
16. 35
17. 85
18. Recession or end of financial year.
19. 235
20. Parent/Teacher

1. (a) 5 mins 45 sec
   (b) 7 mins 6 sec
   (c) 37 seconds
   (d) 2 hr 50 min 12 sec
   (e) 1 hr 15 min 33 sec
   (f) 4 hr 45 min 4 sec
2. (a) 0:56:00 Stopwatch (b) 6:32:00 Stopwatch (c) 15:27:09 Stopwatch
   (d) 21:08:72 Stopwatch (e) 43:19:31 Stopwatch (f) 6:00:43 Stopwatch
3. (a) 3 min 13 sec
   (b) 4 min 5 sec
   (c) 3 hr 10 min 18 sec
   (d) 1 hr 17 min 15 sec

4. £9.30
5. 70 pence
6. 45 pence a pair
7. Same value and price
8. Whole salami
9. £9.54
10. £8.59
11. (a) (b) (c)
12. 72 (a gross is 144)
13. 7 = VII
    29 = XXIX
    13 = XIII
    82 = LXXXII

UNIT 14

1. £280
2. £84
3. £222.50
4. £110
5. Parent/Teacher
6. (a) Card provided by a lender that allows you to use their money for a short period.
   (b) Card provided by a store to buy things in that store on credit.
   (c) Written order for a bank to pay an amount of money from the writer's account.
   (d) Machine where plastic cards can be used to withdraw cash
   (e) A charge for looking after an account.
7. $\frac{3}{8}$ or £30
8. $\frac{1}{8}$ or £10
9. £20
10. £20
11. £50
12. Parent/Teacher
13. 5 metres
14. 6 metres
15. 6 metres
16. Parent/Teacher

1. Two million one hundred and six thousand seven hundred and forty-two.
2. Nine million three hundred and thirty thousand eight hundred and sixteen.
3. Ninety-eight million eight hundred and seventy-one thousand four hundred and twenty three.
4. 4 761 319
5. 8 025 106
6. 69 508 651
7. 4 000 000 + 700 000 + 80 000 + 4 000 + 600 + 3
8. 50 000 000 + 1 000 000 + 300 000 + 50 000 + 9 000 + 200 + 40 + 7
9. 34 601 879, 34 601 789, 31620 714, 31 260 525, 31 260 255

10. A regular benefit usually paid by the government.
11. Money paid in the event of death of an insured policy holder.
12. Paying for goods over a period of time.
13. Goods set aside until paid for.
14. (a) £60
    (b) £90
    (c) £150
15. (a) £20
    (b) £80
16. (a) 14 805 102
    (b) 98 800 008
17. 65E

UNIT 15

1. £9 996.10
2. £6 187.14
3. £9 147.25
4. £9 455.64
5. £23 616.51
6. £7 347.87
7. 11 100km
8. 11 094
9. 5 836m

13.

14.

15.

1. (a) Parent/Teacher
   (b) Parent/Teacher
   (c) Parent/Teacher
   (d) Parent/Teacher
2. (a) 7 min 23 sec 19 hun
   (b) 1 min 11 sec 81 hun
   (c) 9 min 48 sec 33 hun
3. (a) To start again.
   (b) The scale used to measure time.
   (c) Time lost.
   (d) Distance around a circuit or track.
   (e) Mistake made by the user.
   (f) Start or move off before time.

4. £11 039.82
5. £5 156.63
6. £13 871.72
7. £7 281.90
8. 13.172km
9. 13 637tonnes
10. 5.675km
11. 70km/h
12. $3\frac{1}{2}$hours
13. 4:25:60 Stopwatch
14. £90
15. £48

UNIT 16

1. 64 963
2. 155 777
3. 273 930
4. 109 726
5. 245 186
6. 86 559
7. 260 356
8. £2 082 848
9. £338 145
10. 10 094mm
11. 113 179
12. (a) 84311 + 604 + 9832 + 50436 = 145183
    (b) 90648 + 96 + 76504 + 8970 = 176218

13.

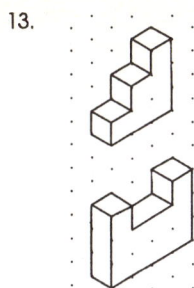

14.

1. (a) $6cm^2$
   (b) $8cm^2$
   (c) $10cm^2$
   (d) $28cm^2$
   (e) $18cm^2$
   (f) $24cm^2$
2. (a) Parent/Teacher
   (b) Parent/Teacher
   (c) Parent/Teacher
   (d) Parent/Teacher
   (e) Parent/Teacher
3. 100m
4. $2m^2$
5. $5\ 400m^2$

6. $45m^2$
7. $117m^2$
8. $72m^2$
9. 44m
10. $88m^2$
11. 39 000l
12. 3 000l
13. 26hrs
14. 113 563
15. 154 204
16. 1 215 239
17. 1 725 278
18. 1 010 346
19. 933 290

UNIT 17

1. 1 000
2. 3 000
3. 2 600
4. 1 431
5. 148
6. 6 615
7. 2 211
8. 4 032
9. 1 689
10. 34 years
11. 1 169 years
12. 1 503 years
13. 6 332km
14. 3 914m
15. Parent/Teacher
16. 4
17. 3
18. 0
19. 2
20. 3

1. Parent/Teacher
2. Parent/Teacher
3. (a) Parent/Teacher
   (b) Parent/Teacher
   (c) Parent/Teacher
   (d) Parent/Teacher
   (e) Parent/Teacher
   (f) Parent/Teacher
4. $24m^3$
5. Parent/Teacher - $1m^3$

6. 1 102
7. 4 211
8. 10
9. 1 818
10. 889
11. 2 520
12. 1 898
13. 1 402
14. 1 674
15. 2 397
16. £119.85
17. Parent/Teacher
18. 50
19. (a) XXXIX
    (b) LVIII
    (c) CXL
    (d) DV

UNIT 18

1. 1 087
2. 289
3. 1994
4. 889
5. 2 889
6. 937
7. 255min
8. £1 125
9. £611
10. 281km
11. 28 948
12. 6740 - 5631 = 1109
13. 5649 - 4538 = 1111
14. 9437 - 7348 = 2089
15. £199.62 - 184.71 = £ 14.91
16. £989.87 - 898.92 = £ 90.95

17.

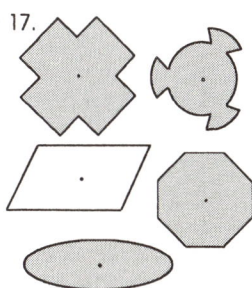

18. (a) Parent/Teacher
    (b) Parent/Teacher
    (c) Parent/Teacher

1. (a) 1ml
   (b) 1g
   (c) 1 000ml
   (d) 1kg
2. (a) 400g
   (b) 750g
   (c) 1.5kg
3. 2kg
4. (a) Parent/Teacher
   (b). Parent/Teacher
   (c) Parent/Teacher
   (d) Parent/Teacher
5. Parent/Teacher
6. One litre of water has a weight of 1 kilogram . Volume and weight are linked.
7. 1 000 litres
8. 35 000 litres

9. 5kg
10. 3.75kg
11. $7\frac{1}{2}$l
12. 4.75kg
13. 3
14. Twice
15. 4 069
16. 892
17. 1 728
18. 6 631
19. 6 984
20. 4
21. 1 110 - Parent/ Teacher
22. 3 595
23. £5 360

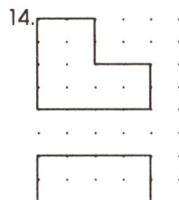

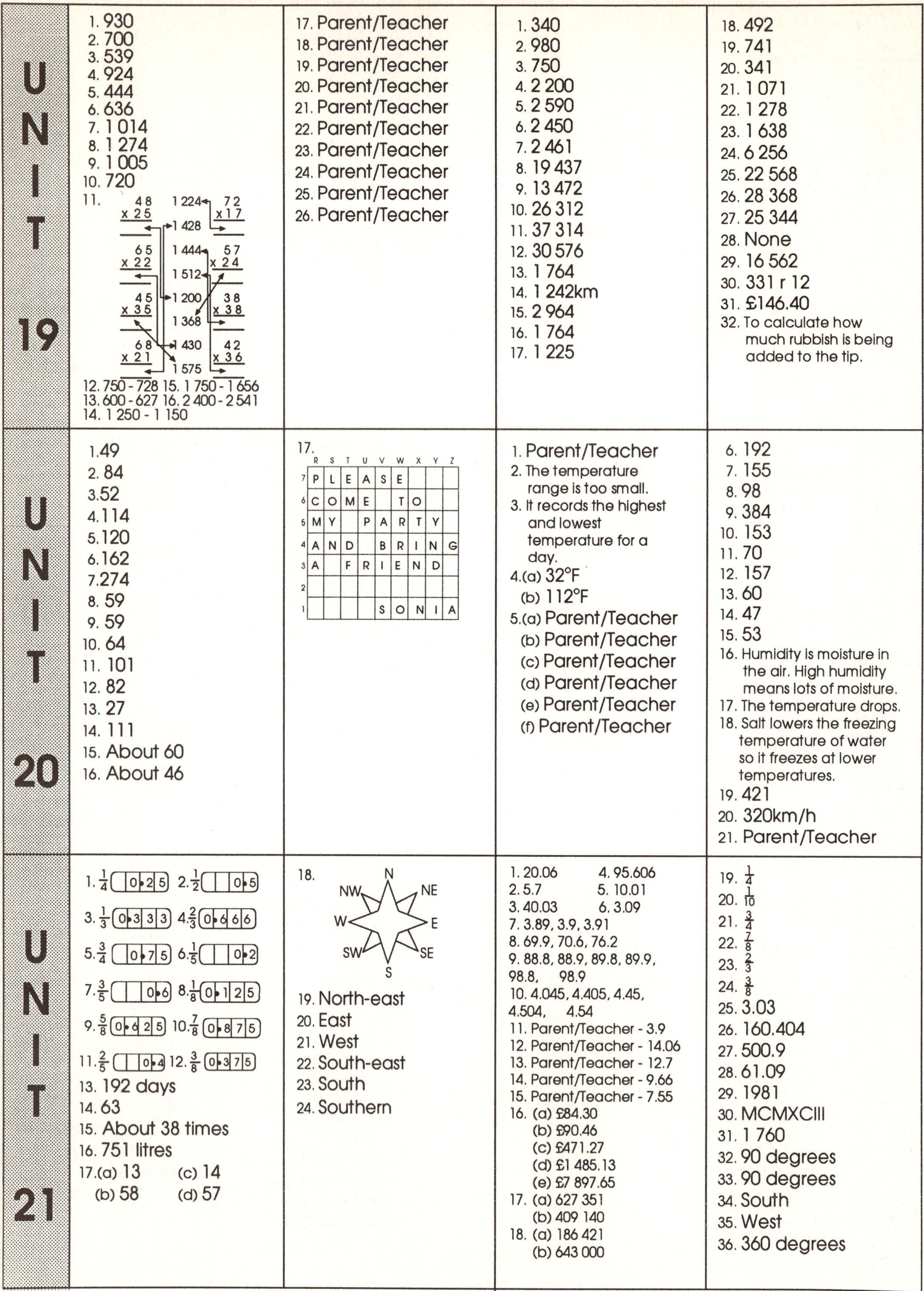

UNIT 19

1. 930
2. 700
3. 539
4. 924
5. 444
6. 636
7. 1 014
8. 1 274
9. 1 005
10. 720
11.

48 x 25	1 224	72 x 17
	1 428	
65 x 22	1 444	57 x 24
	1 512	
45 x 35	1 200	38 x 38
	1 368	
68 x 21	1 430	42 x 36
	1 575	

12. 750 - 728
13. 600 - 627
14. 1 250 - 1 150
15. 1 750 - 1 656
16. 2 400 - 2 541
17. Parent/Teacher
18. Parent/Teacher
19. Parent/Teacher
20. Parent/Teacher
21. Parent/Teacher
22. Parent/Teacher
23. Parent/Teacher
24. Parent/Teacher
25. Parent/Teacher
26. Parent/Teacher

1. 340
2. 980
3. 750
4. 2 200
5. 2 590
6. 2 450
7. 2 461
8. 19 437
9. 13 472
10. 26 312
11. 37 314
12. 30 576
13. 1 764
14. 1 242km
15. 2 964
16. 1 764
17. 1 225
18. 492
19. 741
20. 341
21. 1 071
22. 1 278
23. 1 638
24. 6 256
25. 22 568
26. 28 368
27. 25 344
28. None
29. 16 562
30. 331 r 12
31. £146.40
32. To calculate how much rubbish is being added to the tip.

UNIT 20

1. 49
2. 84
3. 52
4. 114
5. 120
6. 162
7. 274
8. 59
9. 59
10. 64
11. 101
12. 82
13. 27
14. 111
15. About 60
16. About 46
17.

	R	S	T	U	V	W	X	Y	Z
7	P	L	E	A	S	E			
6	C	O	M	E		T	O		
5	M	Y		P	A	R	T	Y	
4	A	N	D		B	R	I	N	G
3	A		F	R	I	E	N	D	
2									
1					S	O	N	I	A

1. Parent/Teacher
2. The temperature range is too small.
3. It records the highest and lowest temperature for a day.
4. (a) 32°F
   (b) 112°F
5. (a) Parent/Teacher
   (b) Parent/Teacher
   (c) Parent/Teacher
   (d) Parent/Teacher
   (e) Parent/Teacher
   (f) Parent/Teacher

6. 192
7. 155
8. 98
9. 384
10. 153
11. 70
12. 157
13. 60
14. 47
15. 53
16. Humidity is moisture in the air. High humidity means lots of moisture.
17. The temperature drops.
18. Salt lowers the freezing temperature of water so it freezes at lower temperatures.
19. 421
20. 320km/h
21. Parent/Teacher

UNIT 21

1. $\frac{1}{4}$ [| 0•2 | 5]
2. $\frac{1}{2}$ [| | 0•5]
3. $\frac{1}{3}$ [0•3 | 3 | 3]
4. $\frac{2}{3}$ [0•6 | 6 | 6]
5. $\frac{3}{4}$ [| 0•7 | 5]
6. $\frac{1}{5}$ [| | 0•2]
7. $\frac{3}{5}$ [| | 0•6]
8. $\frac{1}{8}$ [0•1 | 2 | 5]
9. $\frac{5}{8}$ [0•6 | 2 | 5]
10. $\frac{7}{8}$ [0•8 | 7 | 5]
11. $\frac{2}{5}$ [| | 0•4]
12. $\frac{3}{8}$ [0•3 | 7 | 5]
13. 192 days
14. 63
15. About 38 times
16. 751 litres
17. (a) 13 (b) 58 (c) 14 (d) 57
18. N, NE, E, SE, S, SW, W, NW
19. North-east
20. East
21. West
22. South-east
23. South
24. Southern

1. 20.06
2. 5.7
3. 40.03
4. 95.606
5. 10.01
6. 3.09
7. 3.89, 3.9, 3.91
8. 69.9, 70.6, 76.2
9. 88.8, 88.9, 89.8, 89.9, 98.8, 98.9
10. 4.045, 4.405, 4.45, 4.504, 4.54
11. Parent/Teacher - 3.9
12. Parent/Teacher - 14.06
13. Parent/Teacher - 12.7
14. Parent/Teacher - 9.66
15. Parent/Teacher - 7.55
16. (a) £84.30
    (b) £90.46
    (c) £471.27
    (d) £1 485.13
    (e) £7 897.65
17. (a) 627 351
    (b) 409 140
18. (a) 186 421
    (b) 643 000

19. $\frac{1}{4}$
20. $\frac{1}{10}$
21. $\frac{3}{4}$
22. $\frac{7}{8}$
23. $\frac{2}{3}$
24. $\frac{3}{8}$
25. 3.03
26. 160.404
27. 500.9
28. 61.09
29. 1981
30. MCMXCIII
31. 1 760
32. 90 degrees
33. 90 degrees
34. South
35. West
36. 360 degrees

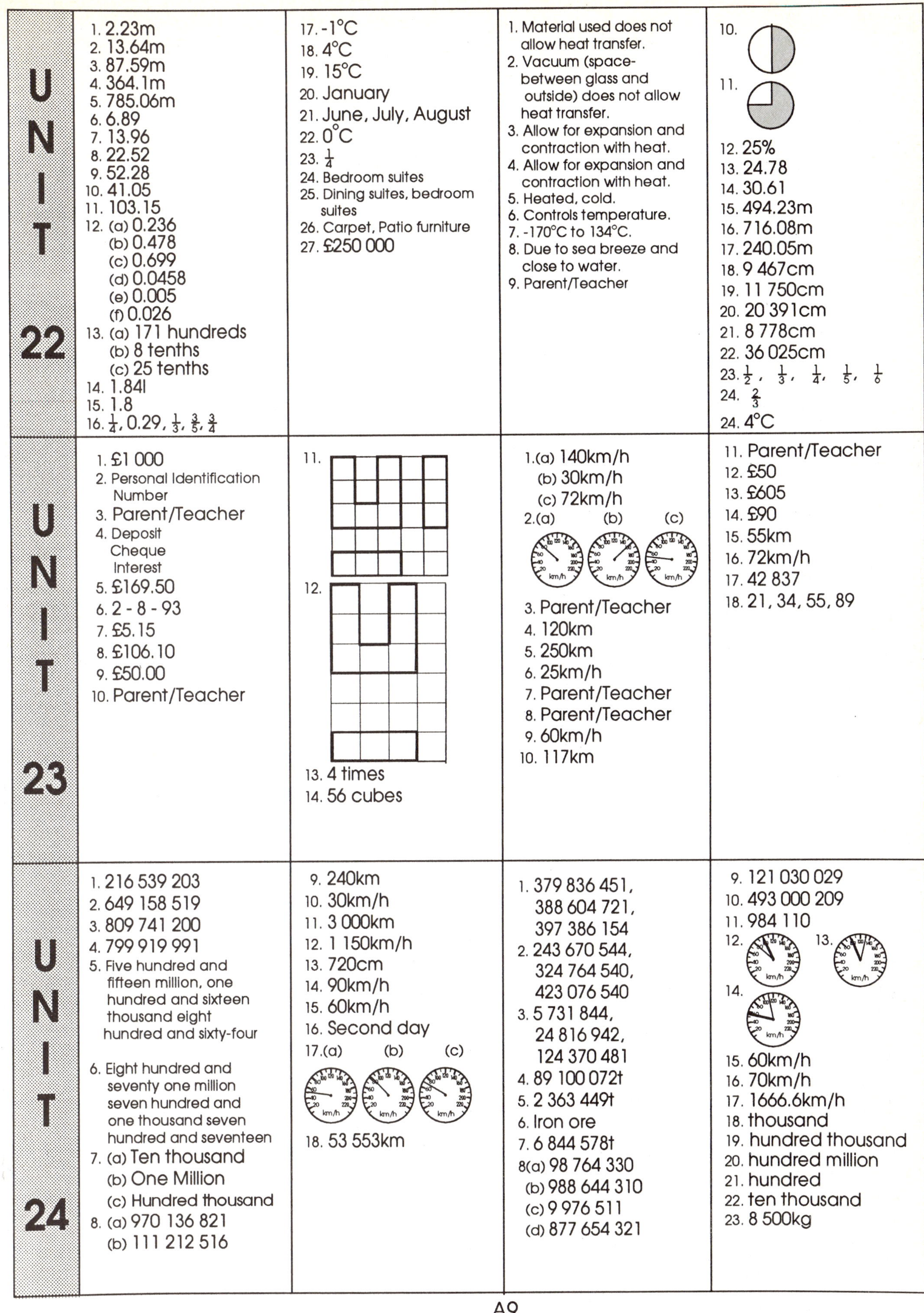

UNIT 22

1. 2.23m
2. 13.64m
3. 87.59m
4. 364.1m
5. 785.06m
6. 6.89
7. 13.96
8. 22.52
9. 52.28
10. 41.05
11. 103.15
12. (a) 0.236
    (b) 0.478
    (c) 0.699
    (d) 0.0458
    (e) 0.005
    (f) 0.026
13. (a) 171 hundreds
    (b) 8 tenths
    (c) 25 tenths
14. 1.841
15. 1.8
16. $\frac{1}{4}$, 0.29, $\frac{1}{3}$, $\frac{3}{5}$, $\frac{3}{4}$

17. -1°C
18. 4°C
19. 15°C
20. January
21. June, July, August
22. 0°C
23. $\frac{1}{4}$
24. Bedroom suites
25. Dining suites, bedroom suites
26. Carpet, Patio furniture
27. £250 000

1. Material used does not allow heat transfer.
2. Vacuum (space-between glass and outside) does not allow heat transfer.
3. Allow for expansion and contraction with heat.
4. Allow for expansion and contraction with heat.
5. Heated, cold.
6. Controls temperature.
7. -170°C to 134°C.
8. Due to sea breeze and close to water.
9. Parent/Teacher

10.
11.
12. 25%
13. 24.78
14. 30.61
15. 494.23m
16. 716.08m
17. 240.05m
18. 9 467cm
19. 11 750cm
20. 20 391cm
21. 8 778cm
22. 36 025cm
23. $\frac{1}{2}$, $\frac{1}{3}$, $\frac{1}{4}$, $\frac{1}{5}$, $\frac{1}{6}$
24. $\frac{2}{3}$
24. 4°C

UNIT 23

1. £1 000
2. Personal Identification Number
3. Parent/Teacher
4. Deposit
   Cheque
   Interest
5. £169.50
6. 2 - 8 - 93
7. £5.15
8. £106.10
9. £50.00
10. Parent/Teacher

11.
12.
13. 4 times
14. 56 cubes

1. (a) 140km/h
   (b) 30km/h
   (c) 72km/h
2. (a) (b) (c)
3. Parent/Teacher
4. 120km
5. 250km
6. 25km/h
7. Parent/Teacher
8. Parent/Teacher
9. 60km/h
10. 117km

11. Parent/Teacher
12. £50
13. £605
14. £90
15. 55km
16. 72km/h
17. 42 837
18. 21, 34, 55, 89

UNIT 24

1. 216 539 203
2. 649 158 519
3. 809 741 200
4. 799 919 991
5. Five hundred and fifteen million, one hundred and sixteen thousand eight hundred and sixty-four
6. Eight hundred and seventy one million seven hundred and one thousand seven hundred and seventeen
7. (a) Ten thousand
   (b) One Million
   (c) Hundred thousand
8. (a) 970 136 821
   (b) 111 212 516

9. 240km
10. 30km/h
11. 3 000km
12. 1 150km/h
13. 720cm
14. 90km/h
15. 60km/h
16. Second day
17. (a) (b) (c)
18. 53 553km

1. 379 836 451, 388 604 721, 397 386 154
2. 243 670 544, 324 764 540, 423 076 540
3. 5 731 844, 24 816 942, 124 370 481
4. 89 100 072t
5. 2 363 449t
6. Iron ore
7. 6 844 578t
8. (a) 98 764 330
   (b) 988 644 310
   (c) 9 976 511
   (d) 877 654 321

9. 121 030 029
10. 493 000 209
11. 984 110
12.
13.
14.
15. 60km/h
16. 70km/h
17. 1666.6km/h
18. thousand
19. hundred thousand
20. hundred million
21. hundred
22. ten thousand
23. 8 500kg

UNIT 25

1. 14 846
2. 14 623
3. 15 406
4. 26 180
5. 31 658
6. 31 780
7. 11 350
8. 26 739
9. 4 497 million km
10. 43 673km^2
11. 8 370mm

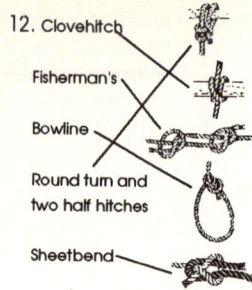

12. Clovehitch
Fisherman's
Bowline
Round turn and two half hitches
Sheetbend

13.(a) Granny knot
14.(a) Parent/Teacher
(b) Parent/Teacher

1.(a) 35mm
(b) 53mm
(c) 18mm
(d) 29 mm
(e) 12mm
2.(a) Parent/Teacher
(b) Parent/Teacher
(c) Parent/Teacher
(d) Parent/Teacher
(e) Parent/Teacher
(f) Parent/Teacher
3.(a) 2cm
(b) 35.6cm
(c) 175cm
(d) 91.9cm
(e) 15cm
(f) $\frac{1}{2}$cm
4.(a) 150mm
(b) 103mm
(c) 171 mm

5. 250mm
6.(a) 47mm
(b) 17mm
(c) 48mm
7. 95mm
8. Parent/Teacher
9. Parent/Teacher
10. Parent/Teacher
11. Bowline
12. 11 867
13. 21 679
14. 27 562
15. £46 435.82
16. £122 214.33

UNIT 26

1. £12 662.28
2. £14 309.89
3. £22 880.48
4. £9 836.65

```
5.  74816      6.    481
    10342          31926
    57276           4507
  + 29591        + 90828
   ------         ------
   172025         127742

7.  98747      8.  31263
    83790          44378
    79348          17875
  + 89487        + 42036
   ------         ------
   351372         135552
```

9. 10 853
10. 16 113m
11. 28 568
12. 109 469

13. Parent/Teacher

14. Parent/Teacher

1. 5 121
2. 7 111
3. 2 035
4. 1884
5. 887
6. 3 082
7. 4 490
8. 87
9. 5 809
10. 1 085km
11. £156
12. £286
13. 3189
14. 1 756
15. £2 684.80
16. £8 383.67

17. 10%
18. 2 089
19. 1 609
20. 9 875
21. 391
22. 9 908
23. £360
24. £210
25. £855
26. £412
27. £540
28. 299m
29. 278kg
30. £2 115
31. 27 016
32. 17 784
33. 110 893
34. Parent/Teacher

UNIT 27

1. 16 844
2. 21 057
3. 51 117
4. 15 392
5. 33 899
6. 77 323
7. 13 515
8. 53 157
9. 15 284
10. 730045
11. 345800
12. 10230
13. £137 245
14. 4 100km
15. £69153.47
16. £18285.90

17. Parent/Teacher

1. (a) $18cm^2$
(b) $60cm^2$
(c) $56cm^2$
2. (a) Parent/Teacher
(b) Parent/Teacher
3. $14cm^2$
4. 8 cm^2
5. $12cm^2$
6. Parent/Teacher

7. (a) Parent/Teacher
(b) Parent/Teacher
(c) Parent/Teacher
8. (a) 6cm
(b) 7cm
(c) 9cm
9. Parent/Teacher-Fill the 3l bottle. Pour from it to fill the 2l bottle. 1l should remain.
10. 27 108
11. 45 226
12. 555
13. 21 265
14. 8 878
15. 1 697
16. 3 596km

UNIT 28

1. 24 206
2. 14 314
3. 23 940
4. 30 870
5. 66458
6. 39788
7. 82 280
8. 80 901
9. 40 061
10. 21 330
11. £6 631
12. 143982km
13. Parent/Teacher - 1 450
14. Parent/Teacher - 1 440
15. Parent/Teacher - 1 225
16. Parent/Teacher - 7 140
17. Parent/Teacher- 2 622
18. Parent/Teacher- 3 822
19. N, NNE, NE, ENE, E, ESE, SE, SSE, S, SSW, SW, WSW, W, WNW, NW, NWN
20. Parent/Teacher
21. Parent/Teacher
22. Parent/Teacher
23. Magnetic properties
24. From the West

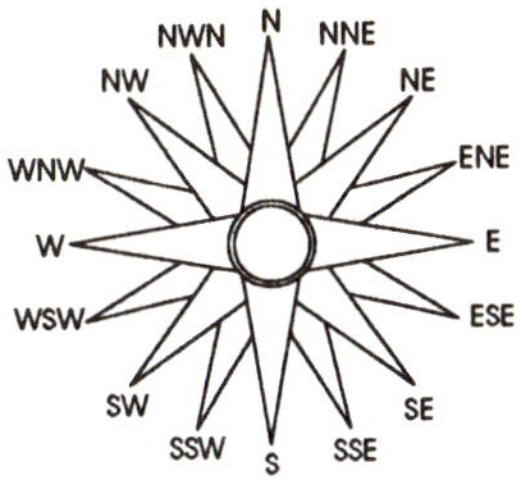

1. 1t
2. 9t
3. 7.5t
4. 4.75t
5. 10t
6. 2.25t
7. 7 500kg
8. 8 500kg
9. 4 700kg
10. 1 9 650kg
11. Parent/Teacher
12. Parent/Teacher
13. 14.5t
14. Parent/Teacher- 802t
15. Facing south
16. Parent/Teacher
17. To North
18. To South
19. Magnet
20. 4 981t
21. (a) kg (b) g (c) g (d) kg (e) t (f) g (g) t
22. 57 204
23. 51 048
24. 78 605
25. 34 692
26. 54 145
27. 32 592
28. Sun

UNIT 29

1. 236 320
2. 59 840
3. 560 880
4. 118 494
5. 321 131
6. 872 102
7. 327 675
8. 136 269
9. 421 400
10. 420 396
11. 360 900
12. 364 500
13. 39 000
14. 8 760
15. 73 440
16. 7 155l
17. 57 240km
18. 160°C - 180°C
19. 200°C - 220°C
20. 180°C - 200°C
21. 140°C - 160°C
22. 30°C
23. Parent/Teacher
24. (a) Parent/Teacher
    (b) Tropical fish need temperature to be maintained evenly.
25. 18 - 23°C
26. Parent/Teacher
27. Body temperature varies over a small range

1. 70.9
2. 81.2
3. 99.4
4. 67.1
5. 237.8
6. 309.0
7. 115.9
8. 95.9
9. 102.5
10. 106.4
11. 0.13
12. 0.03
13. 0.77
14. 0.31
15. 0.56
16. 0.98
17. 89
18. (a) $\frac{1}{4}$ (b) $\frac{2}{5}$ (c) $\frac{1}{3}$ (d) $\frac{3}{4}$ (e) $\frac{3}{5}$ (f) $\frac{83}{500}$
19. 48 864
20. 99 138
21. 143 173
22. 458 337
23. 450 064
24. About 4°C
25. Plastic will not break with expansion.
26. Parent/Teacher
27. 102 725km
28. 266l
29. 9339l
30. 20
31. £5 500

UNIT 30

1. 183.50
2. 23 597
3. 192.17
4. 98.35
5. 112.00
6. [182] - 182.4
7. [128] - 127.8
8. [140] - 140.3
9. [84] - 83.75
10. [86] - 86.9
11. 109
12. 145
13. 83 hour 20 min
14. (a) NNW
    (b) NE
    (c) NW
    (d) ENE
    (e) SE
    (f) S
    (g) SE
    (h) WSW
15. SW
16. SSE, S
17. W
18. 2 500m

1. Parent/Teacher - to measure humidity
2. Temperature; 20, 25, 30, 35, 40, 45, 50; 01:00, 03:00, 05:00, 07:00, 09:00, 11:00, 13:00, 15:00, 17:00, 19:00, 21:00, 23:00
3. 1300hrs
4. 40°C
5. 50°C
6. 27°C
7. 40.75°C
8. 146
9. 186 104
10. 1 216
11. 210 057
12. 110
13. 462 960
14. 1990
15. 1968
16. 9 364.44
17. 469
18. 288 504
19. 610 980
20. 463 156
21. 1 461
22. 187.25
23. 786
24. 5240.41
25. 76.36
26. 182.875
27. Parent/Teacher

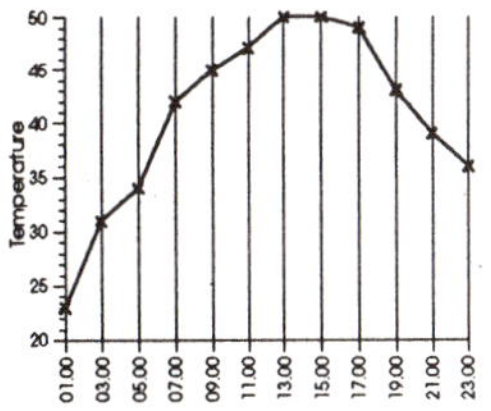

UNIT 31

1. 61
2. 91.7
3. 74.4
4. 130.6
5. 130.9
6. 100.7
7. 209.4
8. 184.9
9. 69. 4
10. 146.7
11. 78.6
12. 154.8
13. 6.2km
14. £78.80
15. 12.5 pence
16. 8.5l/100km
17. About 4.5l

18.(a) Parent/Teacher
(b) Parent/Teacher
(c) Parent/Teacher
19. Parent/Teacher
20. A Mőbius strip has only one side.
21. The strip becomes double the size.
22. Named after a German mathematician (1790-1868).

1. 27.8
2. 76.8
3. 68.52
4. 203.83
5. 126.48
6. 274.14
7. 45.61
8. 137.76
9. 178.61
10. 960.71
11. 5.8 seconds
12. £3.30
13. 3.15l
14. 3.9km

15. 100
16. Yes
17. 200
18. 10km
19. No
20. 0.5ha
21. 500kg
22. $304m^2$
23. £6 066.10
24. £9 619.98
25. £2 648.36
26. £4 118.83
27. £793.65
28. £1 448.88

UNIT 32

1. Parent/Teacher
2. Parent/Teacher
3. Yes. The retailer pays a percentage on all credit card sales.
4. They are adjusted to pounds according to the exchange rate.
5. Goods are exchanged without money changing hands.
6. Parent/Teacher

7. Parent/Teacher
8. Parent/Teacher
9. Parent/Teacher

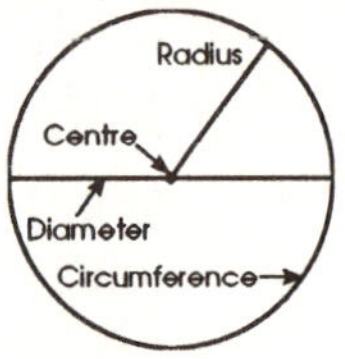

Radius
Centre
Diameter
Circumference

10. 6cm
11. Double
12. Parent/Teacher
13. 90 degrees
14. 360°
15. Parent/Teacher
16. Square
17. Infinite
18. Yes

1. Parent/Teacher
2. The times are earlier as you move west.
3. To take advantage of longer summer days.
4. Usually April to September.
5. 24 hours - 1 day
6. $365\frac{1}{4}$ days
7. No
8. Parent/Teacher

9. Teacher
10.

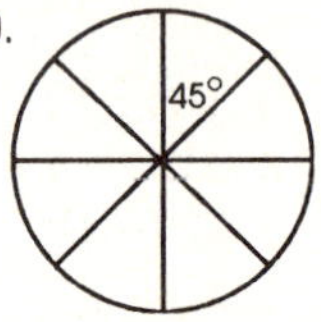

45°

11. 8 parts
12. Octagon
13. You are in debt.
14. You are in credit.
15. 5 hours
16. 0035 Monday   1357 Monday   2059 Sunday

UNIT 33

1. Parent/Teacher
2. A security provided for money lent to buy a property. Legal document.
3. 10%
4. £400
5. £220
6. £2 000
7. per year (each year)
8. £220

9. Parent/Teacher
10. They all add to 180°
11. Parent/Teacher
12. Parent/Teacher

1.(a) 39mm
(b) 64mm
(c) 58mm
2.(a) Parent/Teacher
(b) Parent/Teacher
(c) Parent/Teacher
3.(a) 0.935m
(b) 2.183m
(c) 7.046m
(d) 1.11m
4. Parent/Teacher
5. Parent/Teacher
6. About 40mm
7. About 160mm

8. Parent/Teacher

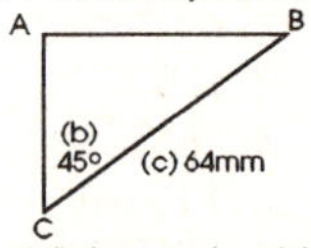

A B C (b) 45° (c) 64mm

(d) Isosceles triangle
(e). 180°

9. 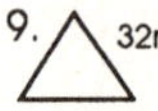 32mm All sides and angles equal

10.

mm	cm	m
980	98	0.98
1 200	120	1.2
1 750	175	1.75

11. $52.80
12. 20%

UNIT 34

1. 21 289
2. 156 953
3. 170 227
4. 170 160
5. 195 744
6. 90 780
7. 12 974
8. 4 324
9. 45 746
10. 15 248
11. 19 338km
12. Nile - Africa
    Amazon - S. America
    Mississippi
    Missouri - N. America

13.	14.	15.
7896	3946	272
402	9674	2536
+ 3717	+ 3268	+ 6984
12015	16888	9792

16. $12cm^2$
17. $144cm^2$
18. $336mm^2$ or $3.36cm^2$
19. $18cm^2$
20. $400mm^2$
21. (a) $8cm^2$
    (b) $6cm^2$
    (c) $15cm^2$
22. 8 000 m^2

1. £1 002.86
2. £1 587.80
3. £8 597.92
4. £27 655.35
5. £108 110.14
6. Parent/Teacher
7. 4 725 runs
8. 34 818
9. A survey of randomly selected people - to collect their opinions on a specific topic.
10. 149 711km^2
11. 1 959km^2
12. Parent/Teacher
    10 276

13. 60cm
14. 1 617m^2
15. 335m^2
16. 2 minutes 26 seconds
17. 150 tonnes
18. £43 532.27
19. £119 905.88
20. £80 403.48
21. £82 352.42
22. (a) 13 hectares
    (b) 10 hectares
23. 92 898
24. 19   21   24

UNIT 35

1.

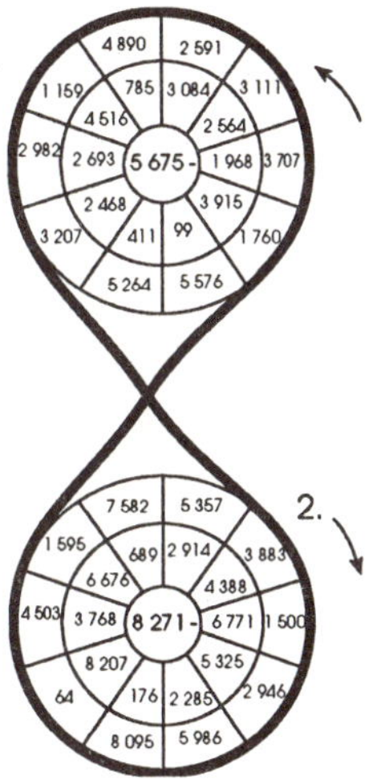

2.

3. 1 227
4. 1 822
5. Parent/Teacher
   1 533

6. Parent/Teacher
7. 45°
8. 45°
9. 90°
10. 180°
11. (a) 112.5°
    (b) 202.5°
    (c) 292.°5
    (d) 22.5°
12. North
13. ENE - 67.5°
14. Circle showing the 32 main compass points. It looks like a rose.

1. £2 405.25
2. £2 412.41
3. £6 698.62
4. 969.07
5. £927.36
6. £61 090.48
7. 210 889
8. 7 892
9. 1 795
10. 1 366km
11. 34 565km
12. 175 382
13. 3 650km/h

14. SSW
15. ESE
16. 67.5°
17. WNW
18. 44 111
19. 228 111
20. 180 527
21. 586 143
22. £1 714.92
23. £7 578.35
24. (a) VII
    (b) LXXXIX
    (c) CXX
    (d) DCXXXV
    (e) MXDI
    (f) DXVI
25. (a) 13cm
    (b) 11.5cm

UNIT 36

1. 13
2. 130
3. 31.3
4. 131.3
5. 60
6. 630
7. 368
8. 3 670
9. 378
10. 2 709
11. 13.96
12. 100.4
13. £25 000
14. 4 356mm - 4.356m
15. 5°C
16. (a) 2 275   (b) 50 090
    (c) 7 400
17. 25.34
18. 72.24
19. 36. 72
20. 29.8

21. Parent/Teacher
22. Parent/Teacher

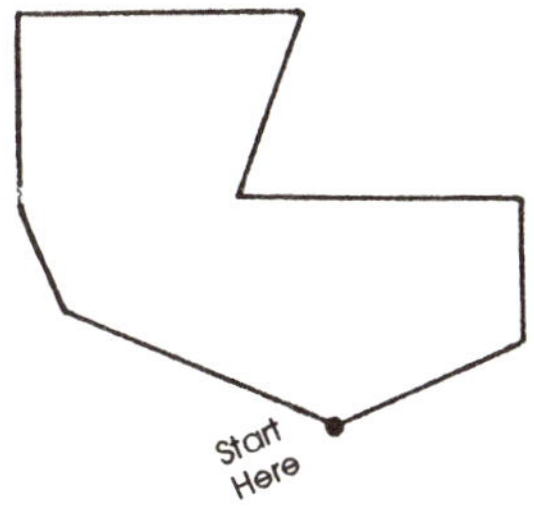

Start Here

1. Parent/Teacher
2. Parent/Teacher
3. Parent/Teacher
4. Parent/Teacher
5. Parent/Teacher
6. Parent/Teacher
7. (a) 1l
   (b) 0.5l
   (c) 15ml
   (d) 20ml
   (e) 500ml
   (f) 2 tonnes
   (g) 750cm^3
8. Litres
9. 3 .5ml
10. 40ml
11. 10ml
12. Parent/Teacher

13. 250 x 187.5m
14. 46 875m^2
15. Parent/ Teacher - Forty metres from the SE corner on the Eastern boundary
26. (a) Parent/Teacher
    (b) Parent/Teacher
    (c) Parent/Teacher
    (d) Parent/Teacher
    (e) Parent/Teacher
    (f) Parent/Teacher
    (g) Parent/Teacher
    (h) Parent/Teacher

UNIT 37

1. 5.6
2. 3.13
3. 6.53
4. 3.23
5. 2.8
6. 8.18
7. £54
8. £111
9. £90
10. 50%
11. £50
12. 24.95
13. 7.91
14. 4.51
15. 4.87
16. 3.3
17. £45.93
18. Nothing
19. Parent/Teacher
20. 3 times
21. Twice
22. About 6%
23. Parent/Teacher

1. Parent/Teacher - about 1 tonne
2. Parent/Teacher
3. Parent/Teacher
4. Parent/Teacher 80kg
5. Parent/Teacher 60kg
6. Parent/Teacher 70kg
7. 21 tonnes
8. 12 tonnes
9. (a) 1.75t
   (b) 19.02t
   (c) 0.48t
   (d) 36.163t
10. (a) 14
    (b) $6\frac{1}{2}$
11. 75
12. 380
13. 60
14. 210
15. 600
16. 576
17. $66\frac{2}{3}$%
18. $\frac{1}{6}$
19. $\frac{1}{3}$
20. 150
21. 300
22. (a) 2.789t
    (b) 14.806t
    (c) 9.96t
23. (a) 15 500kg
    (b) 9 560kg
    (c) 11 010kg
24. 212
25. 50km/h
26. 69.83
27. 25.23
28. 86.76

UNIT 38

1. £34 500
2. £18 330
3. £403. 55
4. £438.15
5. 3 600
6. £11 390
7. Parent/Teacher
8. Parent/Teacher
9. 110
10. 260
11. 1991
12. 1988
13. 1992
14. 105
15. 1994 - 260
    1995 - 230
16. 10
17. 13
18. Parent/Teacher 10

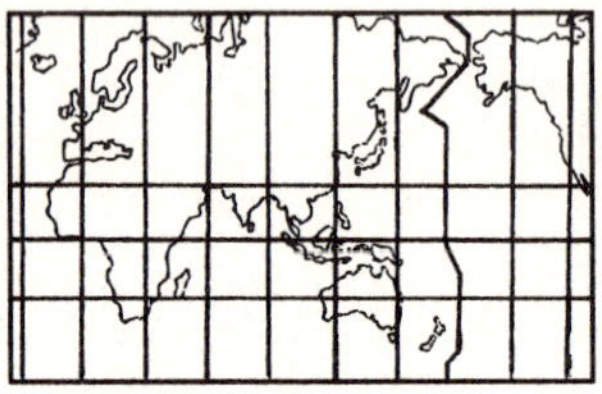

2. When day and night are equal in length.
3. The shortest and longest days of the year.
4. About 21st June
5. Time from which all other times are taken.
6. (a) 8.00 a.m.
   (b) 5.00 a.m.
   (c) 3.00 a.m
   (d) Monday 10.00 p.m.
   (e) Saturday 11.00 p.m

7. Where company shares are bought and sold.
8. Agent who buys and sells shares.
9. £1 625
10. 2 years
11. 10p.m.
12. $7 601.79
13. 1 089.86
14. 8 170.2
15. 12.08
16. 628.2
17. 20 454
18. 15 6 21
19. 1908
20. £600
21. (a) 45°
    (b) 60°

Notes

Notes

Notes

Find these **answers** without using a calculator.

1. 34×10 = ______
2. 49×20 = ______
3. 25×30 = ______
4. 55×40 = ______
5. 37×70 = ______
6. 49×50 = ______

You may use a calculator for these.

7. 107×23 = ______
8. 341×57 = ______
9. 421×32 = ______
10. 572×46 = ______
11. 691×54 = ______
12. 784×39 = ______

13. An airline runs 36 flights, each with 49 passengers. How many passengers altogether? ______

14. A marathon runner runs 46km per day for 27 days. How far does she run altogether? ______

15. At a concert, 39 rows of seats each hold 76 people. How many people are seated? ______

16. Sixty-three sacks of onions have a weight of 28kg each. What is the total weight? ______

17. A bus holds 49 passengers. If there are 25 buses going to a show, how many people go by bus? ______

Use a calculator if you need it.

18. 12 x 41 = ______
19. 13 x 57 = ______
20. 11 x 31 = ______
21. 17 x 63 = ______
22. 18 x 71 = ______
23. 42 x 39 = ______
24. 68 x 92 = ______
25. 56 x 403 = ______
26. 48 x 591 = ______
27. 36 x 704 = ______

28. How many times will this figure match when it rotates 360°?

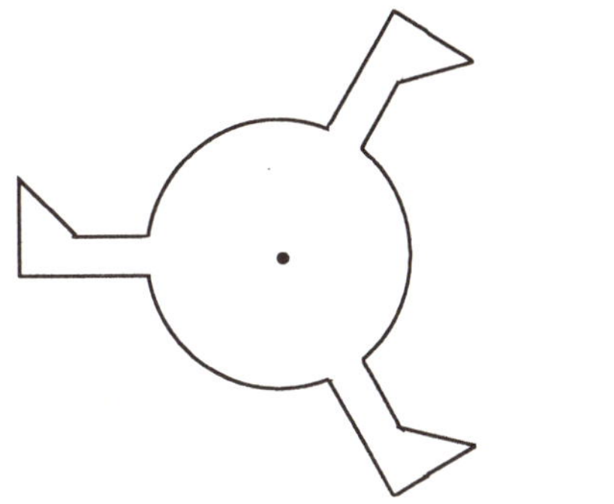

______

29. Ninety-eight apple trees give an average of 169 apples per tree. How many apples in total? ______

30. If the apples were packed 50 to a case - how many cases? ______

How many apples left over? ______

31. Over five weeks a worker earns £172, £134, £181, £118 and £127. What were the average weekly earnings? ______

32. There is a weigh bridge at the entrance to a tip. Trucks full of rubbish are weighed as they enter and again when they leave. Why?

______

______

______

______

Use a calculator for these activities. There should be no remainders.

1. 1 127 ÷ 23 = ______
2. 3 024 ÷ 36 = ______
3. 4 056 ÷ 78 = ______
4. 4 788 ÷ 42 = ______
5. 8 280 ÷ 69 = ______
6. 9 234 ÷ 57 = ______

Use a calculator for these activities. Write any remainders to the nearest number.

7. 27) 7 406
8. 48) 2 839
9. 86) 5 078
10. 71) 4 545
11. 64) 6 491
12. 58) 4 757

13. There are **1 755** sheep to be taken to market in a fleet of trucks. If each truck holds **65** sheep, how many trucks are needed? ______

14. A factory packs **24** packets of Oaties into a carton. If there are **2 664** packets, how many full cartons? ______

15. A scientist had **3 542** tadpoles in a **60m³** pond for study. About how many tadpoles per cubic metre? ______

16. Overnight **780** tadpoles turn into frogs. How many tadpoles per cubic metre the next day? ______

17. Sonia gave a party and worked out a fun invitation. This is what she did. Fill it in and decorate with colour.

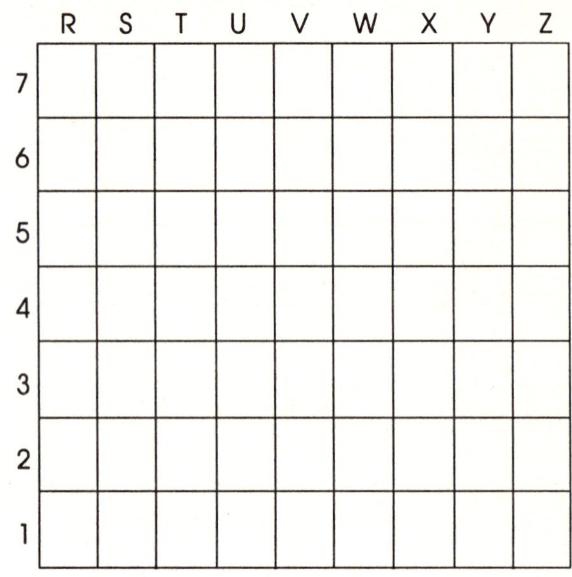

Write the letters of the alphabet on the grid to read the invitation.

A *U7 V5 R4 R3 Z1*
B *V4*
C *R6*
D *Y3 T4*
E *T7 W7 U6 W3*
F *T3*
G *Z4*
I *X4 V3 Y1*
L *S7*
M *T6 R5*
N *S4 Y4 X3 X1*
O *S6 X6 W1*
P *R7 U5*
R *W5 W4 U3*
S *V7 V1*
T *W6 X5*
Y *Y5 S5*

1. List some places where you would find some type of **thermometer** or **temperature** controller in use.

____

____

____

____

____

____

2. Why would a **clinical thermometer** be of no use in recording daily **temperatures?**

____

____

3. How does a **maximum/minimum thermometer** work?

____

____

____

4. Find out about the Fahrenheit temperature scale and then record these temperatures using the scale.

(a) Freezing point of water ________°F

(b) Boiling point of water ________°F

5. Using a **Celsius scale,** what would you expect the approximate temperatures of these to be?

(a) An icecream ________

(b) An electric blanket ________

(c) Hot cup of coffee or tea ________

(d) An oven cooking a cake ________

(e) Summer's day at the beach ________

(f) Winter's day at the North Pole ________

Use a calculator for these sums. Write remainders to the nearest number.

6. 4 032 ÷ 21 = ______ 7. 5 735 ÷ 37 = ______

8. 8 232 ÷ 84 = ______ 9. 7 296 ÷ 19 = ______

10. 6 885 ÷ 45 = ______ 11. 5 040 ÷ 72 = ______

12. 9 420 ÷ 60 = ______ 13. 3 360 ÷ 56 = ______

14. 3 666 ÷ 78 = ______ 15. 4 929 ÷ 93 = ______

16. On a summer's day, the temperature is average, but people are saying the **humidity** is high. What does **humidity** mean?

____

____

17. Using a thermometer, find out what happens when you add salt to ice.

____

____

18. Why is salt added to icy winter roads?

____

____

19. In a country town there are 1 762 telephone lines. Lightning knocks out 1 341 lines. How many still work? ________

20. A plane flew 2 560km in eight hours. What was its average speed? ________

21. Draw a simple three-winged shape that will match three times as it rotates 360°.

Write the way a calculator would show these **fractions.**

1. $\frac{1}{4}$ [ ][ ][ ][ ]
2. $\frac{1}{2}$ [ ][ ][ ][ ]
3. $\frac{1}{3}$ [ ][ ][ ][ ]
4. $\frac{2}{3}$ [ ][ ][ ][ ]
5. $\frac{3}{4}$ [ ][ ][ ][ ]
6. $\frac{1}{5}$ [ ][ ][ ][ ]
7. $\frac{3}{5}$ [ ][ ][ ][ ]
8. $\frac{1}{8}$ [ ][ ][ ][ ]
9. $\frac{5}{8}$ [ ][ ][ ][ ]
10. $\frac{7}{8}$ [ ][ ][ ][ ]
11. $\frac{2}{5}$ [ ][ ][ ][ ]
12. $\frac{3}{8}$ [ ][ ][ ][ ]

13. An astronaut was in orbit for **4 608** hours. How many days was this? ______

14. Geologists are looking for oil over an area of **2 835km²**. They work in smaller areas of **45km²**. How many of these areas are there? ______

15. The United Kingdom has an area of 244 000km². The USA has an area of 9 363 000km². How many times could the **UK** fit inside the **USA?** Write the answer to the nearest whole number. ______

16. A household uses **67 594l** of water in **90 days.** What is the average daily use? Round off the answer. ______

17. Round off, to the nearest whole number, these computer figures.

(a) 13.053 ______ (b) 57. 616 ______

(c) 13. 503 ______ (d) 57. 161 ______

18. Label the eight points of the **compass** .

This is a plan of a holiday centre.

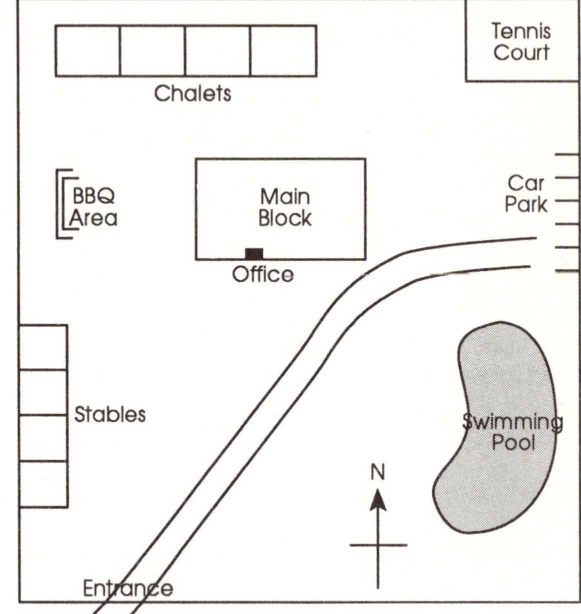

19. In which direction do you go from the entrance to reach the office? ______

20. If you were in one of the chalets, in which direction would you walk to reach the tennis court? ______

21. The barbecue area is to the ______ of the main block.

22. You would head ______ from the office for a swim.

23. The stables are to the ______ of the barbecue area.

24. The entrance is on the ______ boundary of the property.

Put an X on all the **non-significant zeros,** and write each number correctly.

1. 20.060 ________
2. 05.70 ________
3. 040.030 ________
4. 095.606 ________
5. 010.010 ________
6. 3.090 ________

Arrange these numbers in rising order.

7. 3.9, 3.89, 3.91 ________________

8. 70.6, 76.2, 69.9 ________________

9. 98.9 89.8 88.8 89.9 98.8 88.9

____

10. 4.045 4.45 4.54 4.405 4.504

____

Write any number that falls between each pair.

11. 3.91 ________ 3.89

12. 14.05 ________ 14.07

13. 12.76 ________ 12.67

14. 9.64 ________ 9.68

15. 7.5 ________ 7.6

16. Write these pence as pounds and pence, using **decimal notation.**

(a) 8 430 pence ________________

(b) 9 046 pence ________________

(c) 47 127 pence ________________

(d) 148 513 pence ________________

(e) 789 765 pence ________________

17. Add 170 000 to each of these numbers.

(a) 457 351 ________

(b) 239 140 ________

18. Subtract 170 000 from each of these numbers.

(a) 356 421 ______ (b) 813 000 ______

Change these calculator readings into **fractions,** e.g. 0.333 = $\frac{1}{3}$

19. 0•25 ___
20. 0•1 ___
21. 0•75 ___
22. 0•875 ___
23. 0•666 ___
24. 0•375 ___

Write these numbers, without the **non-significant zeros.**

25. 03.030 ________
26. 160.404 ________
27. 500.90 ________
28. 061.09 ________

29. Film credits usually show in Roman numerals the year when the film was made. What year was this?

MCMLXXXI ________

30. If you had to write the year 1993 on a film, what would you write?

____

31. Kew Gardens, London, opened in this year. What is it?

MDCCLX ________

Most maps have a north indicator, something like this. Use it to help calculate directions and angles.

N

32. How many degrees between North and East? ______

33. What is the angle between West and South? ______

34. What direction is immediately opposite North? ______

35. What direction is 180° from East? ______

36. What is the sum of the total angles of a compass? ______

Write these **centimetres** in **metres,** using decimal notation.

1. 223 centimetres ________
2. 1 364 centimetres ________
3. 8 759 centimetres ________
4. 36 410 centimetres ________
5. 78 506 centimetres ________

Add **5.5** to each of these numbers.

6. 1.39 ________ 7. 8.46 ________

8. 17.02 ________ 9. 46. 78 ________

10. 35.55 ________ 11. 97.65 ________

12. Rearrange these sets of numbers, using **decimal points** to make the smallest number possible.
(e.g. 4 079 gives 0.479)

(a) 2 306 ________ (b) 4 780 ________

(c) 9 069 ________ (d) 48 050 ________

(e) 5 000 ________ (f) 6 020 ________

13. Circle the number which is bigger.

(a) 17 tenths or 171 hundredths

(b) 12 hundredths or 8 tenths

(c) 25 tenths or 200 hundredths

14. What is the difference between **81.671 and 79.831?** ________

15. Add these **fractions** and write as a **decimal fraction.**

$$\frac{2}{10} + \frac{30}{100} + \frac{7}{10} + \frac{60}{100} = \_\_\_\_\_\_$$

16. Arrange these fractions, smallest to largest.

$\frac{1}{4}$ $\frac{1}{3}$ 0.29 $\frac{3}{4}$ $\frac{3}{5}$

____

This graph shows average monthly temperatures.

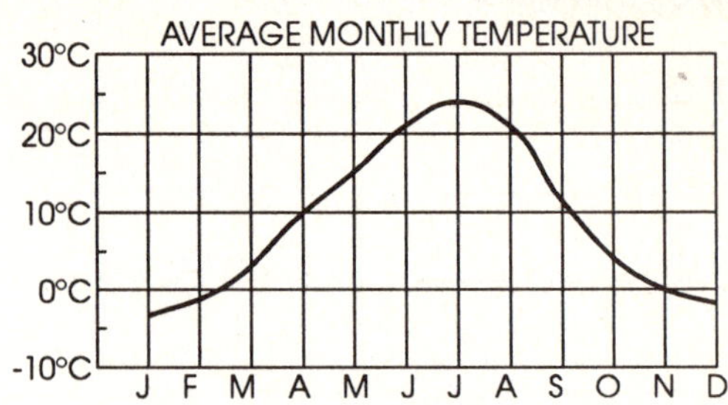

17. What is the average monthly temperature (AMT) for February? ________

18. What is the AMT for October? ________

19. What is the AMT for May? ________

20. Which is the coldest month of the year? ________

21. Which are the three warmest months?

________ ________ ________

22. What is the AMT for November? ________

23. For what fraction of the year is the temperature zero or below? ________

This **pie chart** shows furniture sales for a discount store.

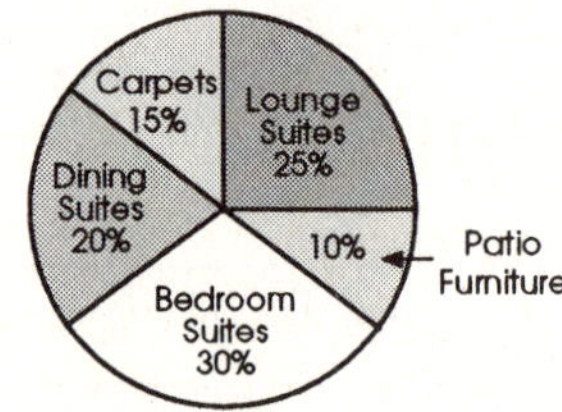

24. Which items of furniture sold most?

____

25. What two groups of furniture make up 50% of the sales?

________ ________

26. Which two groups, when combined, make 25% of the sales?

________ ________

27. If sales total £1 million, what was the value of lounge suites sold? ________

1. How does a cool-bag or cool-box keep things cold or hot?

______

______

2. How does a **vacuum** flask keep things hot or cold?

______

______

3. Did you know that the Sydney Harbour Bridge, Australia, rests on rollers at each end? Why?

______

______

4. Why does a concrete path or road have joins in it?

______

______

5. Many materials **expand** when they are ______ and **contract** when they are ______.

6. What is the function of a thermostat?

______

7. Find out the temperature on the surface of the moon. ______

8. Why are temperatures on the coast cooler in summer than inland?

______

______

9. What were your area's **maximum** and **minimum temperatures** yesterday?

max ______ min ______

10. Show 50% on the **pie chart**, then shade it.

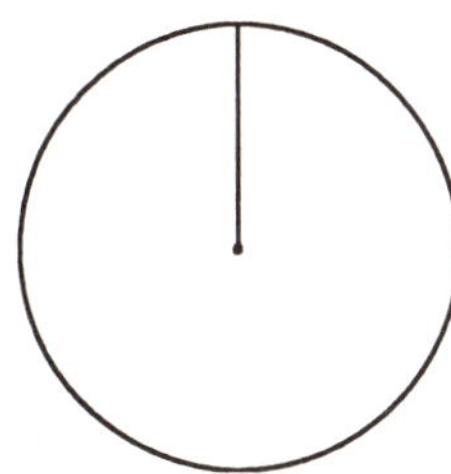

11. Show another **25%** on the **pie chart** and colour it.

12. How much of the chart is not shaded or coloured? ______

Write these **centimetres** as **metres,** using **decimal notation.**

13. 2 478cm ______
14. 3 061cm ______
15. 49 423cm ______
16. 71 608cm ______
17. 24 005cm ______

Write these **metres** as **centimetres.**

18. 94.67m ______
19. 117.5m ______
20. 203.91m ______
21. 87.78m ______
22. 360.25m ______

23. Arrange these **fractions** in order - largest to smallest.

$\frac{1}{3}$ $\frac{1}{4}$ $\frac{1}{8}$ $\frac{1}{2}$ $\frac{1}{5}$

______

24. Circle the **fraction** that comes in the middle of this range.

$\frac{7}{10}$ $\frac{73}{100}$ $\frac{1}{12}$ $\frac{3}{16}$ $\frac{2}{3}$ $\frac{5}{6}$ $\frac{7}{12}$

25. Which is the middle **temperature** in this range?

-13°C 29°C 36°C -7°C 4°C

1. A lady with a **credit card** spends £150 and £75 one month. She still has **available credit** of £775.

   What is her **credit limit?** _______

2. What is a PIN? ________________________________

   ____

3. Some banks allow you to make up your own PIN. What would you choose?

   ____

This is part of a bank statement

Date	Transaction	Credit	Debit	Balance
				169.50
06 07 93	D	25.00		194.50
30 07 93	CASH		0.25	194.25
02 08 93	D	356.00		550.25
12 08 93	C012		83.00	467.25
23 08 93	C013		106.10	361.15
31 08 93	INT	5.15		366.30

4. What do these abbreviations mean?

   D ________________________________

   C ________________________________

   INT ________________________________

5. How much is the opening balance? _______

6. What date was a monthly pay day? _______

7. How much interest was earned? _______

8. How much was the cheque withdrawal 013? _______

9. If you had £1 000 in the bank for one year at 5% interest, how much would you earn? _______

10. The difference between our currency and that of other countries is the exchange rate. What is the exchange rate for $1 US today? _______

11. Draw the **front, side** and **top views** of the cube shape on the small grid.

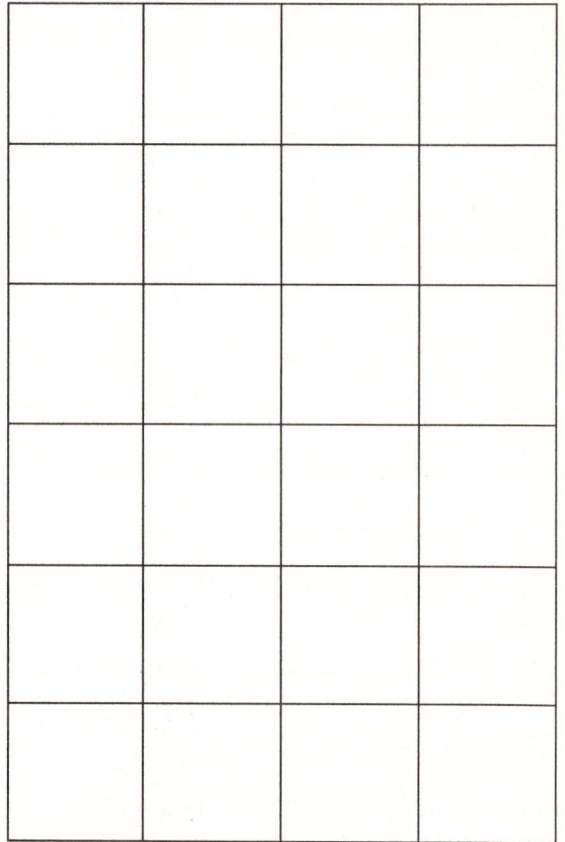

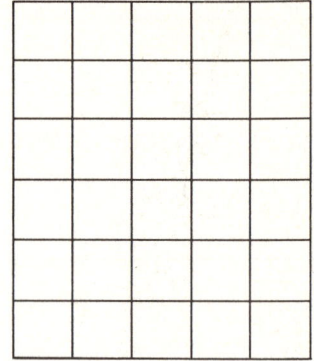

12. Draw the **front** and **top views** of the shape on the larger grid.

13. By **doubling** each side of the **front view,** how much has its **area** been increased? _______

14. If the number of cubes in the **length, width** and **height** of the shape above were doubled, how many cubes would make up the new shape? _______

1. Record the speeds shown on these speedometers.

(a) 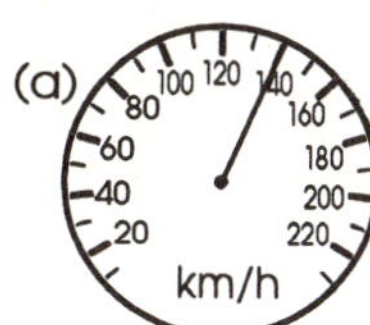 (b) 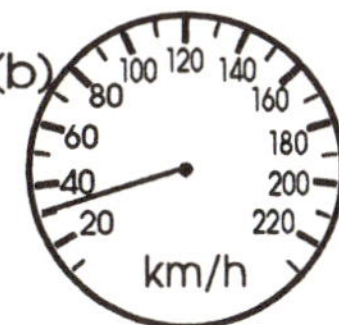 (c) 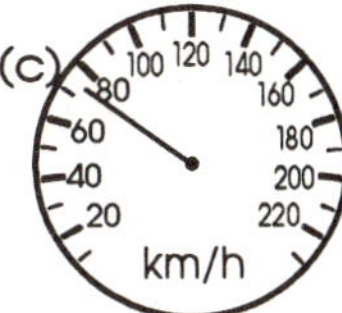

_______ _______ _______

2. Show the speed on each speedometer.

(a) 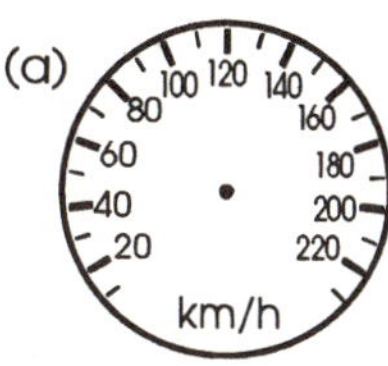 (b) 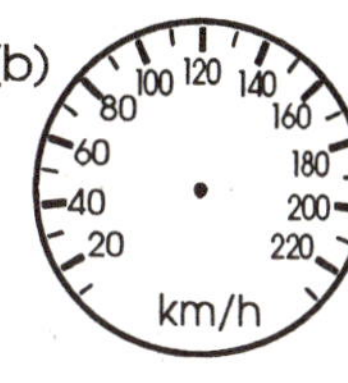 (c) 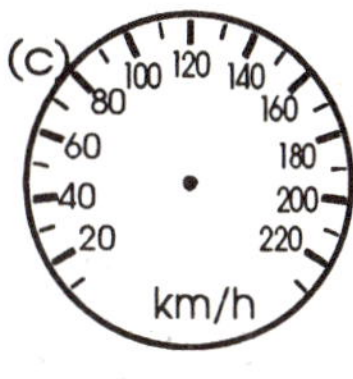

80km/h 160km/h 50km/h

3. What is the speed limit outside your school or home? _______

4. If a car travels at 60 kilometres per hour for two hours, what distance does it cover? _______

5. A plane travels at 500km/h for half an hour. What distance does it cover? _______

6. A cyclist travels for two hours and covers a distance of 50km. At what speed did she travel? _______

7. Fill in three speed limit signs you have seen in your area.

8. Walk one kilometre at normal speed and time yourself. What is your normal walking speed? _______

9. A car travels 180 kilometres in 3 hours. At what average speed does it travel? _______

10. The **odometer** of a car shows distance travelled. It shows **58 261** before a trip. After the trip it shows **58 378.** How far was the trip? _______

11. Make a list of some ways people earn money.

____

____

____

____

____

12. If you **invest** £500 at **10% interest** per annum, what would you expect to earn in a year? _______

13. If you added the **interest** to your £500, what would you have at the end of the second year, in total? _______

14. If you borrowed **£1 000** at **9% interest** per year, what **interest** would you owe at the end of the first year? _______

15. A very fast train travels at **220km/h.** How far would it travel in a quarter of an hour? _______

16. A driver was travelling in a **60km/h** speed zone. The driver was booked for travelling **20%** over the speed limit. How fast was he going? _______

17. The **odometer** of a car showed **43 267** after a trip of **430km.** What was the odometer reading before the trip? _______

18. Find out about **Fibonacci numbers.** Can you add four numbers to the **Fibonacci sequence?**

0 1 1 2 3 5 8 13 ___ ___ ___ ___

Write these words as numbers.

1. Two hundred and sixteen million five hundred and thirty-nine thousand two hundred and three ________

2. Six hundred and forty-nine million one hundred and fifty-eight thousand five hundred and nineteen ________

3. Eight hundred and nine million seven hundred and forty-one thousand two hundred ________

4. Seven hundred and ninety-nine million nine hundred and nineteen thousand nine hundred and ninety-one ________

Write these numbers in words.

5. 515 116 864 ________

6. 871 701 717 ________

7. Give the value for the numbers in bold.

   (a) 489 3**4**5 721 ________

   (b) 37**1** 824 645 ________

   (c) 817 **1**03 733 ________

8. Add 1 500 000 to each number.

   (a) 968 636 821 ________

   (b) 109 712 516 ________

9. A bus travels at **80km/h** for three hours. What distance does it travel? ________

10. Seb rode his bike **15km** in half an hour. What was his speed in km/h? ________

11. Concorde, the supersonic airliner, is able to fly at **2 000km/h.** If it flies for 1.5 hours at this speed, what distance does it cover? ________

12. Find out how fast sound travels. ________

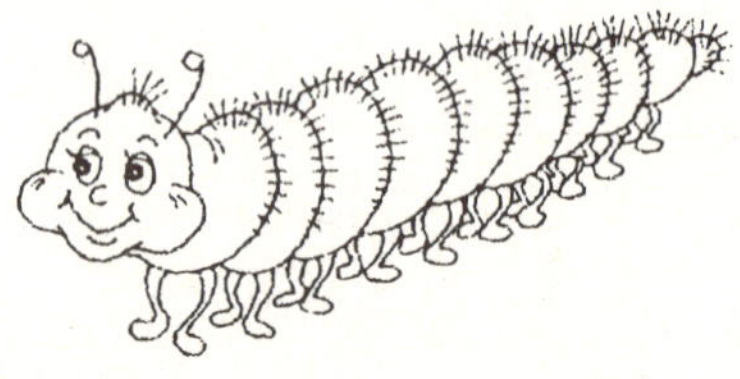

13. A caterpillar crawls at a rate of **12cm** per minute. If it crawls at this speed for an hour, how far will it travel? ________

In a rally, a car travels 450km the first day in 5 hours, and 360km in 6 hours on the second day.

14. What was the car's average speed on the first day of the rally? ________

15. What was the car's average speed on the second day? ________

16. Which day had the tougher conditions? ________

17. Show these average speeds on the speedometers.

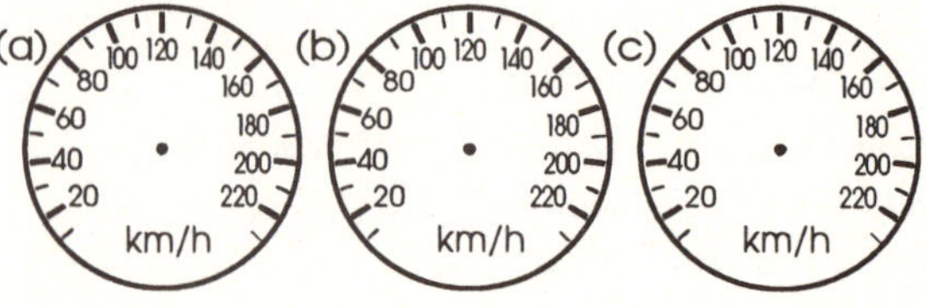

(a) 450km in 9 hours

(b) 40km in half an hour

(c) 210km in 3 hours

18. A car's **odometer** shows 42 153km. If its average travel is 950km per month, what will the odometer read after one more year's motoring? ________

Rearrange each set of numbers in order, smallest to largest.

1. 379 836 451, 397 386 154, 388 604 721

2. 423 076 540, 243 670 544, 324 764 540

3. 24 816 942, 5 731 844, 124 370 481

These were totals of some exports in one year, given in **tonnes.**

	Tonnes
Sugar	***2 523 711***
Wheat	***16 648 685***
Iron Ore	***89 100 072***
Coal	***85 297 940***
Timber	***2 363 449***
Barley	***5 344 578***

4. What was the biggest export that year, in tonnes? ______

5. What was the lowest among those shown here? ______

6. Which was bigger - coal or iron ore?

7. If the export of barley was $1\frac{1}{2}$ million tonnes more last year, what was the tonnage? ______

8. Rearrange each set of numbers to make the largest number possible.

(a) 380176493______

(b) 146340898______

(c) 6119975______

(d) 478361752 ______

Write these words as numbers.

9. One hundred and twenty-one million thirty thousand and twenty-nine ______

10. Four hundred and ninety-three million two hundred and nine ______

11. Nine hundred and eighty-four thousand one hundred and ten ______

12. Show the speedometer reading in red if the car increased speed by 25%.

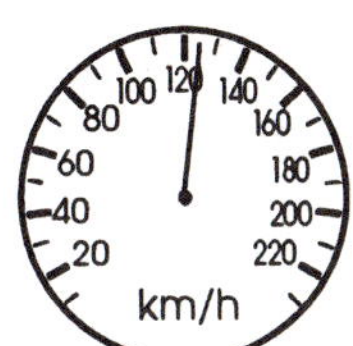

13. Show in red the new speedometer reading if the car reduced its speed by 20%.

14. Show the speedometer reading in red if the car reduced its speed by 50%.

15. A car travels 90km in $1\frac{1}{2}$ hours. What is the car's average speed? ______

16. Another car travels 140km in 2 hours. What is its speed? ______

17. The earth spins 40 000km in 24 hours. Use a **calculator** to find the speed at which it spins. ______

Give the value for the bold numbers.

18. 301 49**6** 547 ______

19. 823 **0**16 009 ______

20. **6**17 823 419 ______

21. 400 938 **2**48 ______

22. 718 9**0**4 351 ______

23. How many kilograms is 82 tonnes? ______

1.
```
  2987
  7194
  3904
+  761
```

2.
```
  8605
   312
  5692
+   14
```

3.
```
   784
  4859
   461
+9302
```

4.
```
  7643
  9877
  3018
+5642
```

5.
```
  4096
 13489
  7241
+6832
```

6.
```
  8163
     9
   460
+23148
```

7. These were the attendances at three sessions of an outdoor rock concert: **2 563, 4 845** and **3 942.** What was the total attendance? _______

8. These cans of drink were sold at the same concerts: **13 496** cans of cola, **6 437** cans of orange and **6 806** cans of lemonade. How many cans sold altogether? _______

9. Moving outwards, Earth's orbit is **150** million kilometres from the sun, Saturn's orbit is **1 277** million kilometres from Earth's and Neptune's is **3 070** million km from Saturn's. How far is Neptune from the sun? _______

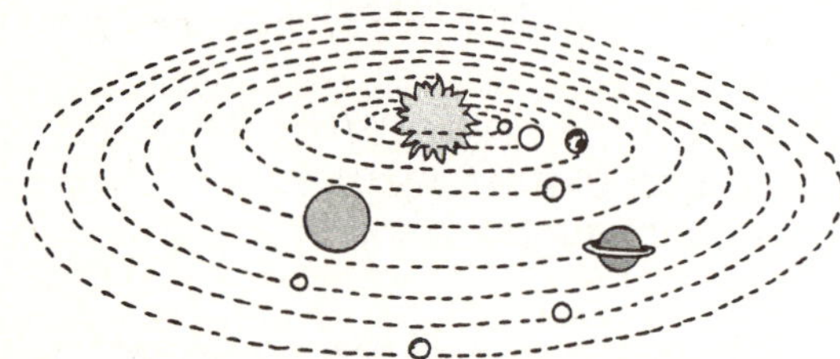

10. These are the areas of four states in the United States:

Delaware ***5 329km²*** *New Jersey* ***20 295km²***

Hawaii ***16 705km²*** *Rhode Is.* ***1 344km²***

What is the total area of the four states? _______

11. In 5 years these were the rainfalls of Greentown: **1 389mm, 2 063mm, 1 785mm, 1 647mm** and **1 486mm.** What was the total rainfall? _______

12. Tie each of these **knots,** and then match the **knot** to its name.

Clove hitch

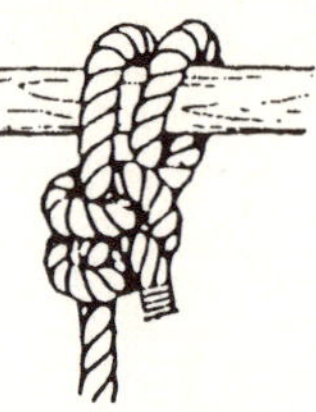

Fisherman's

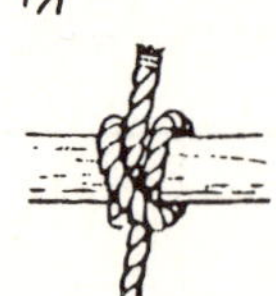

Bowline

Round turn and two half hitches

Sheet bend

13. The first of these knots is the well-known Reef knot. Can you name knot (b)?

(a)  Reef Knot

(b)  _______________

14. Write a possible use for each knot

(a) ______________________________

(b) ______________________________

1. Measure the lengths of these lines in **millimetres.**

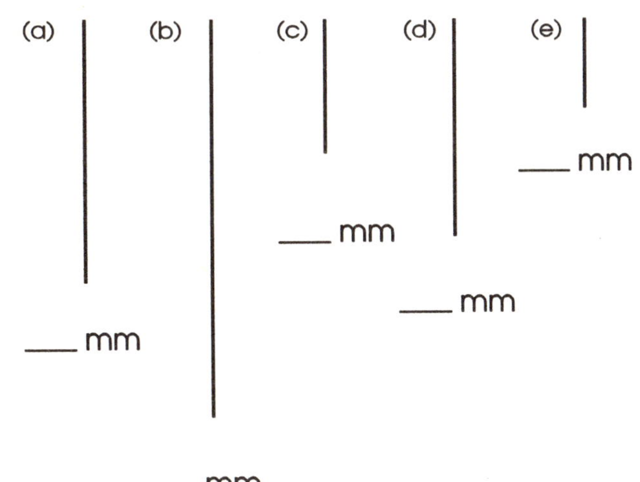

2. Measure these in **millimetres.**

(a) Length of a pencil ________

(b) One side of a stamp ________

(c) Diameter of a 20p coin ________

(d) One of your fingers ________

(e) Perimeter of a bar of soap ________

(f) Height of a drinking glass ________

3. Convert these **millimetre** measurements to **centimetres.**

(a) 20mm ________

(b) 356mm ________

(c) 1 750mm ________

(d) 919mm________

(e) 150mm ________

(f) 5mm ________

4. Measure the **perimeter** of each shape in millimetres (mm).

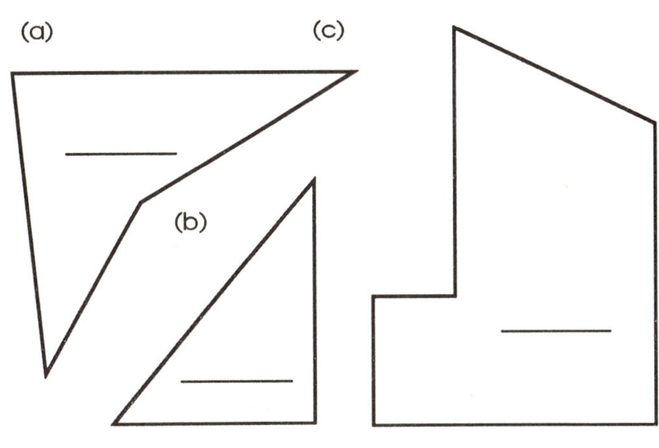

5. Measure the length of the line down the centre of this page in millimetres. ________

6. Measure these lines in **millimetres.**

(a) ________________________ ____ mm

(b) ________ ____ mm

(c) ________________________ ____ mm

7. The average rainfall for Clinton is 1 227mm. If it was only 1 132mm one year, how many millimetres less than the average? ________

8. List three places in the world where rainfall is more than 2 metres per year.

____

____

____

9. Measure the length of a straight pin in millimetres. ________

10. How far across the head of the pin? ________

11. What would be a good knot for tying up a rowing boat?

____

12.	13.	14.
4306	9431	15176
3921	1247	7963
2078	2965	4082
+1562	+8036	+ 341
____	____	____

15.	16.
£14078.62	£17906.27
7796.54	43178.89
19122.57	6542.13
+ 5438.09	+ 54587.04
____	____

1.
```
 £3484.75
   502.82
  2574.29
 +6100.42
 ________

 ________
```

2.
```
 £1748.94
  7609.53
  4176.35
 + 775.07
 ________

 ________
```

3.
```
 £7315.05
  3883.19
  6401.92
 +5280.32
 ________

 ________
```

4.
```
 £ 416.55
  3798.06
   341.72
 +5280.32
 ________

 ________
```

Fill in the mising numbers.

5.
```
   7481_
   10342
   5_276
 + 29591
 _______
  1720_5
 _______
```

6.
```
     481
   3_926
    4507
 + 908_8
 _______
  1_7_4_
 _______
```

7.
```
   98_47
   8379_
   7_348
 + 894_7
 _______
  3_1372
 _______
```

8.
```
   312_3
   4_378
   1787_
 + 42_36
 _______
  1_5552
 _______
```

9. Write the answer to this sum and then make up a story to go with it.

4 728 + 3 649 + 2 091 + 385 = ________

____

____

____

10. Four oil wells are drilled to depths of **3 097m**, **4 640m**, **3 865m** and **4 511m**. What was the total depth of drilling? ________

11. The populations of four neighbouring towns are **5 675** people, **7 363**, **8 145** and **7 385**. What is the total population of the region? ________

12. 83 721 + 6 483 + 19 265 = ________

13. **Slide, flip** and **turn** this basic pattern on the grid to form an attractive **tessellation**.

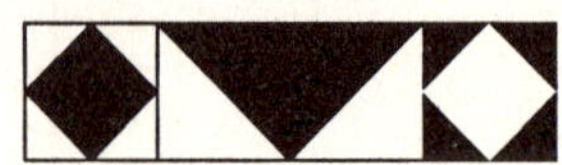

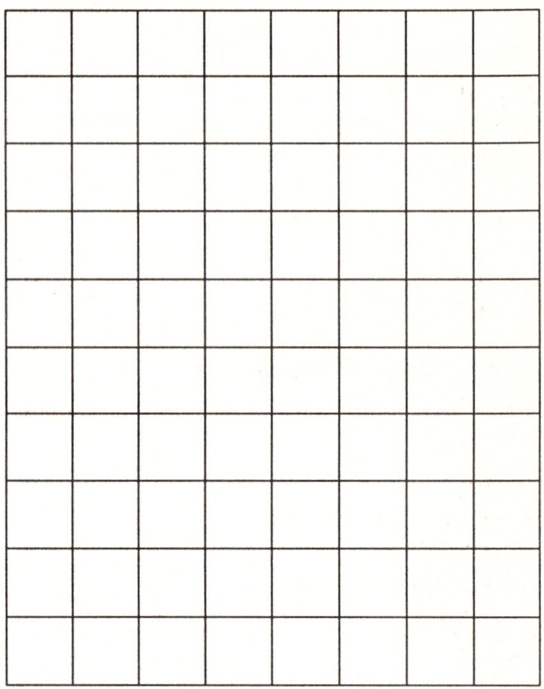

14. **Slide, flip** and **turn** this basic curved pattern on the grid to form an attractive **tessellation**.

1.
```
  5961
-  840
```

2.
```
  7394
-  283
```

3.
```
  6017
- 3982
```

4.
```
  3642
- 1758
```

5.
```
  8593
- 7706
```

6.
```
  7169
- 4087
```

7.
```
  9068
- 4578
```

8.
```
  1976
- 1889
```

9.
```
  9898
- 4089
```

10. If it is **6 315km** from Sydney to Singapore and **7 400km** from Sydney to Hong Kong, how much further is Hong Kong than Singapore? ________

11. A TV and video that normally sell for **£1 695** is discounted to **£1 539**. How much is the saving? ________

12. The regular price of a camcorder is **£1 275**. The sale price is **£989**. What is the saving? ________

13. Attendance at a cricket match was **4 954** on the first day, but on the second day it was **1 765** less. What was the attendance on the second day? ________

14. Complete the sum, then work out a story to go with it.

5 437 - ________ = 3 681

____

____

____

15.
```
£ 4372.77
- 1687.97
```

16.
```
£ 25781.54
- 17397.87
```

17. A computer is advertised for **£2 500**, but is sold at **£2 250**. What was the **percentage discount**? ________

Fill in the gaps.

18. 4 173 - 2 084 = ________

19. 3 042 - ________ = 1 433

20. ________ - 7 589 = 2 286

21. 8 045 - ________ = 7 654

22. ________ - 8 099 = 1 809

Fill in the **discount prices**.

23. £450 discount 20% = ________

24. £840 discount 75% = ________

25. £950 discount 10% = ________

26. £618 discount $33\frac{1}{3}\%$ = ________

27. £900 discount 40 % = ________

28. A hill town has an annual rainfall of **1 256mm**. A seaside town has an average of **957mm**. What is the difference? ________

29. **1 486kg** of potatoes are harvested. **1 208kg** are sold. How many kilograms left unsold? ________

30. A man is buying a boat for **£9 750** but finds he has only **£7 635**. How much will he borrow? ________

31.
```
  6480
  5392
  7043
+ 8101
```

32.
```
  3275
  5637
  8149
+  723
```

33.
```
  84731
    975
   8349
+ 16838
```

34. People talk of a 'cashless society'. Can you think of three things for which you will always need cash?

____

____

____

1. 38492
 - 21648

2. 74105
 - 53048

3. 60749
 - 9632

4. 56304
 - 40912

5. 61008
 - 27109

6. 84328
 - 7005

7. 90000
 - 76485

8. 93157
 - 40000

9. 31611
 - 16327

10. When Captain Phillip sailed into Port Jackson he had with him **747 000** nails for building. If **16 955** were used in the first month, how many were left? ______

11. **840 900** tonnes of grapes were produced in France . **495 100** tonnes were sold for winemaking. How many tonnes were used for other purposes? ______

12. A factory packed **87 560** apples in one shift and **97 790** the next. How many more in the second shift? ______

13. A family bought a house ten years ago for **£146 750**. They want to sell it for **£283 995**. How much profit if they sell the house? ______

14. It is **16 700km** by air from Melbourne to New York and **12 600km** from Melbourne to San Francisco. How far is it from New York to San Francisco? ______

15. £83717.29
 - 14563.82

16. £37985.38
 - 19699.48

17. Make up different tile patterns that will **tessellate**. Then **flip, slide** and **turn** them to make interesting patterns on the grid.

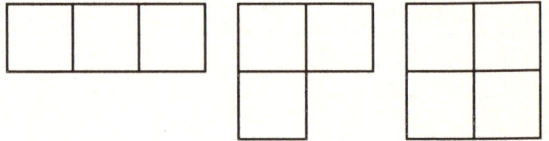

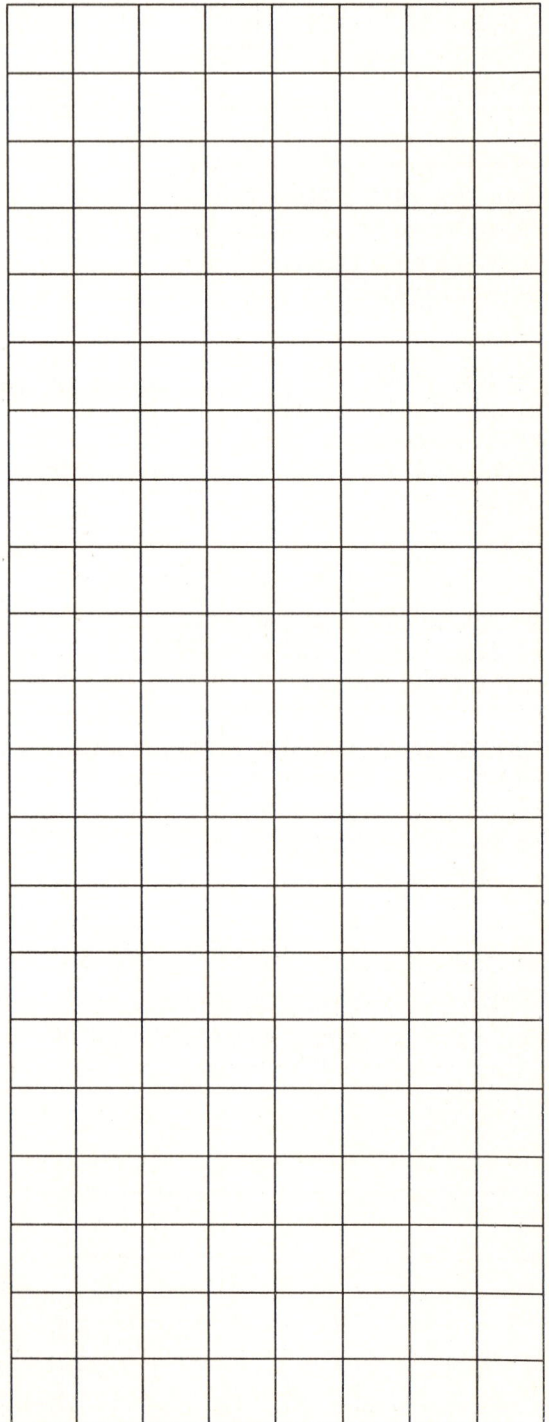

1. Calculate the area of each rectangle.

Length	Width	Area cm²
3cm	6cm	
12cm	5cm	
7cm	8cm	

2. Measure the **length** and **width** of these rectangular shapes and calculate the areas.

(a) A teatowel ________

(b) A car space in a parking area ________

Find the **areas** of these rectangular shapes.

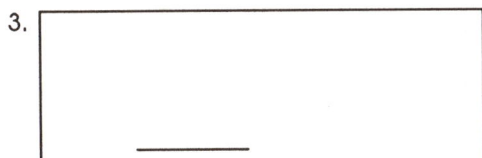

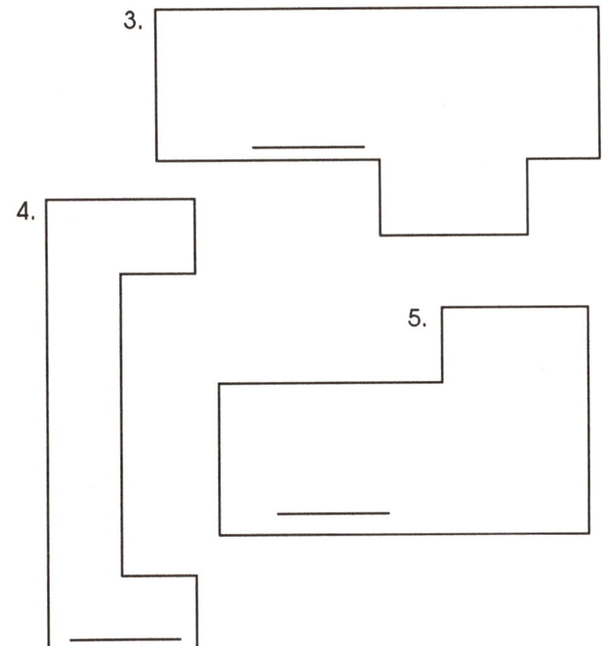

6. Find the **weight** of 4 different containers filled with water. Record their **weight** when full, then empty. Find the difference to calculate the **capacity**.

Container	Weight (filled)	- Weight (empty)	= Weight/ Capacity

7. Give the **dimensions** of three different rectangles all with an area of 200m².

(a) ________ m x ________ m = 200m²

(b) ________ m x ________ m = 200m²

(c) ________ m x ________ m = 200m²

8. Use a scale of **1 cm = 1 m** to find the **areas** of these three shapes in m².

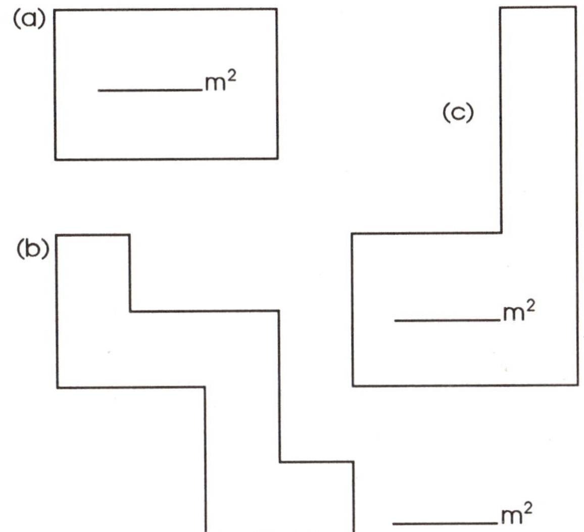

9. You have a **2l** and a **3l** container, but you need to measure out **1l** into another container. How could you do it?

____

____

10. 41706 - 14598 = ________

11. 78185 - 32959 = ________

12. 30432 - 29877 = ________

13. 29047 - 7782 = ________

14. 53726 - 44848 = ________

15. 89676 - 87979 = ________

16. A car clocks up **78 596km** on its odometer. It should have been serviced at **75 000km**. How far past the service is the car? ________

1. 931 x 26 = ______

2. 842 x 17 = ______

3. 630 x 38 = ______

4. 735 x 42 = ______

5. 707 x 94 = ______

6. 686 x 58 = ______

7. 935 x 88 = ______

8. 909 x 89 = ______

9. 413 x 97 = ______

10. A canteen uses **790** bread rolls every day. How many are used in **27** days? ______

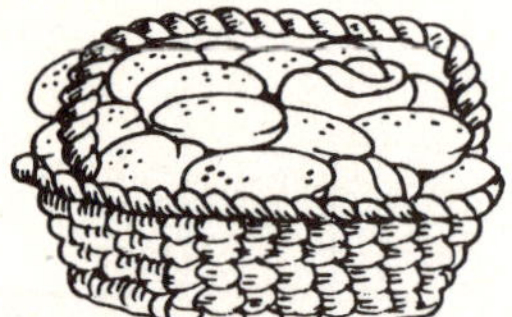

11. A holiday to Florence costs **£349** per person. If a group of **19** people make a booking, how much altogether? ______

12. A truck driver travels **3 789km** each week for **38** weeks. How many kilometres does he travel in total? ______

Estimate the following **products** (results) to a round figure, then check with a calculator.

		Estimate	Calculator Check
13.	50 x 29 =		
14.	96 x 15 =		
15.	49 x 25 =		
16.	85 x 84 =		
17.	57 x 46 =		
18.	39 x 98 =		

19. Fill in the sixteen directional points on the **compass**.

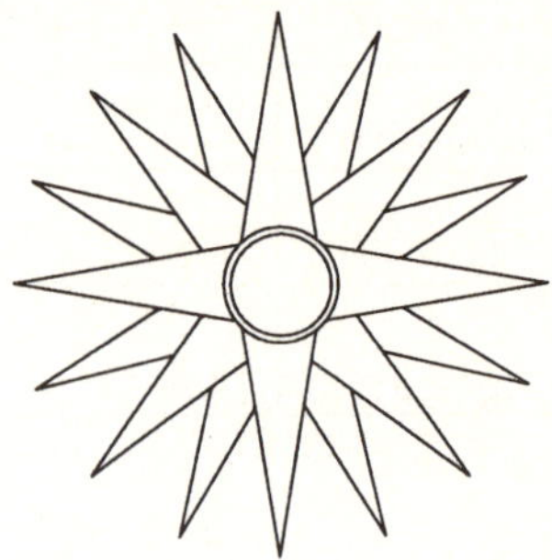

20. Draw a simple plan of the land your school or home stands on and add a **north** point.

21. Find out which **direction** your bedroom window faces. ______

22. List four things that make a **compass needle** swing.

______

______

______

______

23. What do these things have in common?

______

______

24. If someone says : " The wind is a westerly" - from what direction does the wind blow? ______

Write these **weights** in **tonnes**. Use the abbreviation **t**.

1. 1 000kg ______
2. 9 000kg ______
3. 7 500kg ______
4. 4 750kg ______
5. 10 000kg ______
6. 2 250kg ______

Write these **tonnes** in **kilograms**.

7. 7.5t ______
8. 8.5t ______
9. 4.7t ______
10. 19.65t ______

11. List three large objects that have their weight expressed in **tonnes**.

______

______

______

12. List three materials or products usually measured in **tonnes**.

______

______

______

13. A truck unloaded **3 tonnes** of sand at a building site, **5 tonnes** at another site and **6½ tonnes** at a third. How many tonnes of sand did the truck deliver? ______

14. Complete the **sum** and make up a story to go with it.

______

______

______

$$\begin{array}{r} 3740t \\ -\ 2938t \\ \hline \end{array}$$

15. On which side of the house roof would you put a **solar** heater? ______

16. Make a **sundial** on the ground, using a vertical stick at the centre of a circle. Mark the hours during a sunny day.

17. In which direction would the shadow fall at midday on a sunny day here? ______

18. In Australia, in which direction would the shadow fall at midday? ______

19. When using a compass you should always be sure there is no ______ near it.

20. **293** loads of sand are needed for a building site. Each load contains **17t**. How many **tonnes** in all? ______

21. Write the **unit of weight** you would normally use for these materials (**g**, **kg** or **t**).

(a) Bag of cement ______

(b) Headache powder ______

(c) Flour for a cake ______

(d) A large melon ______

(e) Gravel ______

(f) Bird seed ______

(g) Coal ______

22. $\begin{array}{r} 681 \\ \times\ 84 \\ \hline \end{array}$

23. $\begin{array}{r} 709 \\ \times\ 72 \\ \hline \end{array}$

24. $\begin{array}{r} 995 \\ \times\ 79 \\ \hline \end{array}$

25. $\begin{array}{r} 826 \\ \times\ 42 \\ \hline \end{array}$

26. $\begin{array}{r} 637 \\ \times\ 85 \\ \hline \end{array}$

27. $\begin{array}{r} 679 \\ \times\ 48 \\ \hline \end{array}$

28. What is the nearest star to Earth? ______

1. 6 7 5 2
 x 3 5
 ______

2. 1 4 9 6
 x 4 0
 ______

3. 7 3 8 0
 x 7 6
 ______

4. 2 0 4 3
 x 5 8
 ______

5. 4 7 9 3
 x 6 7
 ______

6. 8 8 9 9
 x 9 8
 ______

7. 4 369 x 75 = ______

8. 5 047 x 27 = ______

9. 8 600 x 49 = ______

10. 7 932 x 53 = ______

11. 4 010 x 90 = ______

12. 3 645 x 100= ______

13. A Southern Fried Chicken shop sells about **1 500** chicken legs each week. How many chickens would this require for a year? ______

14. At port Bizzi, ships go in and out at the rate of **24** per day. How many ships is this in a year? ______

15. A nursery sends **3 060** bunches of tulips to the flower market. If each bunch has **24** in it, how many tulips in all? ______

16. A taxi's petrol tank holds **45l**. It is filled **159** times in a year. How many litres of petrol does it use in that year? ______

17. If the taxi does **8km** to the **litre**, how many **kilometres** is that? ______

Give an approximate **temperature** for each of the following.

18. A moderate oven ______

19. A hot oven ______

20. A moderately hot oven ______

21. A low oven ______

22. The **temperature** of hot tap water is about **70°C**. By how many **degrees** does it need to rise before it boils? ______

23. Draw the sort of **thermometer** you might see in a car.

24. (a) Draw an aquarium **thermometer**.

(b) Why is an exact **temperature** so important in an aquarium?

(a) (b) ______

______

______

______

______

25. What is a pleasant **temperature** range for a swimming pool? ______

26. Draw a suitable scale on the clinical **thermometer**.

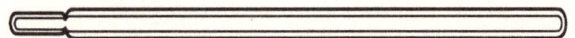

27. Why is the **temperature range** so short?

______

______

Use a calculator to complete each sum. Write the answers to one **decimal place**. The first one is done for you.

1. 7) 496 = 70.9
2. 9) 731
3. 40) 3 975
4. 90) 6 037
5. 33) 7 849
6. 27) 8 342
7. 55) 6 374
8. 61) 5 847
9. 47) 4 817
10. 86) 9 153

Write these calculator readings to two **decimal places**. The first one is done for you.

11. 0.126 **0.13**
12. 0.033 ________
13. 0.768 ________
14. 0.307 ________
15. 0.555 ________
16. 0.976 ________

17. There are **7 565** jellybeans. They can be packed in bags of **85.** How many bags? ________

18. Write these calculator readings as **fractions**.

(a) 0.25 ________
(b) 0.4 ________
(c) 0.333 ________
(d) 0.75 ________
(e) 0.6 ________
(f) 0.166 ________

19. 2 036 x 24 = ________

20. 3 198 x 31 = ________

21. 4 937 x 29 = ________

22. 8 041 x 57 = ________

23. 9 784 x 46 = ________

24. What is the recommended temperature for storage of milk? ________

25. Why is an ice-cube tray made of plastic and not glass?

____

____

26. Give an example of things rubbing together and becoming hot.

____

27. A car covers **2 935km**. The owner says he will trade it in when it covers 35 times that distance. What will the odometer read then? ________

28. If the car does **11km** to a **litre** of petrol, how many **litres** has he used to the present time? ________

29. How many **litres** will it have used by the time it is traded in? ________

30. The car has its oil changed every **5 000km**. How many oil changes will it have had by the time it is traded in? ________

31. The car cost **£13 750**.The owner hopes to trade it in for **40%** of that price. What amount would that be? ________

Unit 30

Use a calculator for these divisions and write the answers to **two decimal places**.

1. 5 872 ÷ 32 = ________
2. 6 843 ÷ 29 = ________
3. 9 032 ÷ 47 = ________
4. 8 360 ÷ 85 = ________
5. 4 368 ÷ 39 = ________

In each of the following select the most suitable answer of the three choices by writing over the dotted line. Check with a calculator and write in the answer.

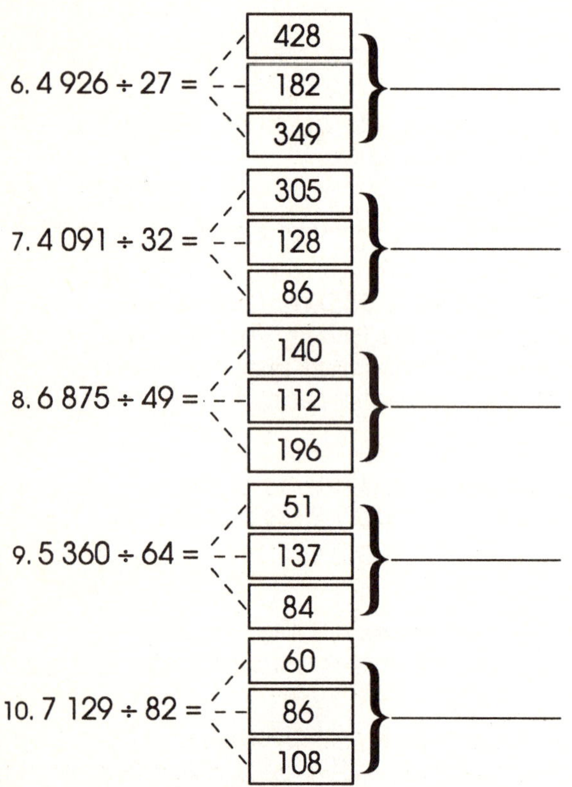

6. 4 926 ÷ 27 =
428
182
349
7. 4 091 ÷ 32 =
305
128
86
8. 6 875 ÷ 49 =
140
112
196
9. 5 360 ÷ 64 =
51
137
84
10. 7 129 ÷ 82 =
60
86
108

11. A golfer scored **2 616** for **24** rounds. How many did he average per round? ________

12. Benjamin arranged his 3 335 stamps equally into 23 albums. How many in each? ________

13. If a cyclist averages **36km/h**, how long will it take to cycle **3 000km?** ________

This is an orienteering course at Bush Hill.

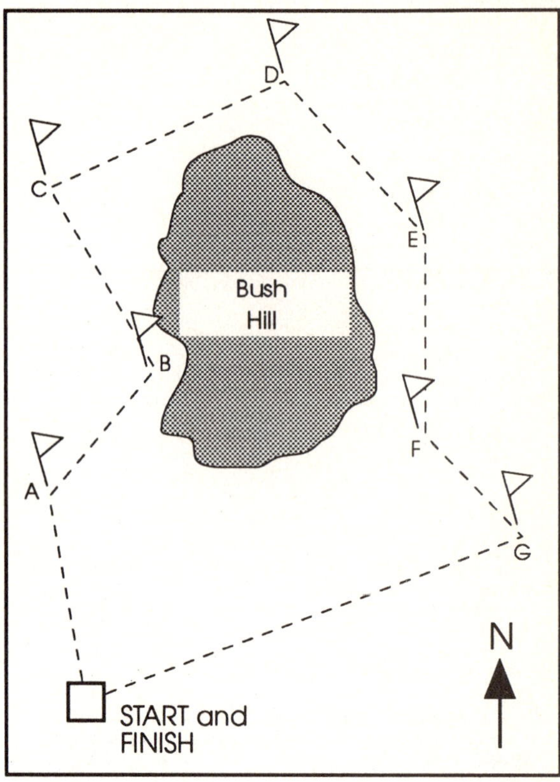

14. Fill in the directions to go with the map of the orienteering course.

(a) Start to A ________ (b) A to B ________

(c) B to C ________ (d) C to D ________

(e) D to E ________ (f) E to F ________

(g) F to G ________ (h) G to finish ________

15. A competitor sprains her ankle at E and decides to go directly back to the finish. In what direction will she go? ________

16. Another competitor leaves E and arrives at G instead of F. He must have gone ________ instead of ________.

17. In what direction is Bush Hill from E? ________

18. If the course map at Bush Hill is to a scale **1cm = 100m**, what is the length of the course in km? ________

1. How does a **wet and dry thermometer** work and for what is it used?

____

____

____

This is a table of **temperatures** recorded over a 24 hour period.

Time	Temperature	Time	Temperature
01.00hrs	23°C	13.00hrs	50°C
03.00hrs	31°C	15.00hrs	50°C
05.00hrs	34°C	17.00hrs	49°C
07.00hrs	42°C	19.00hrs	43°C
09.00hrs	45°C	21.00hrs	39°C
11.00hrs	47°C	23.00hrs	36°C

2. Show each **temperature** with a small x and join them to make a **graph**.

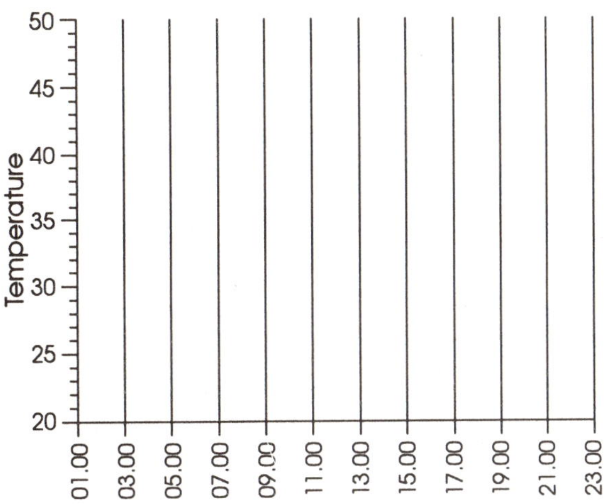

3. At what time did the **temperature** peak? ________

4. What would the **temperature** have been at 20.00 hours? ________

5. What would the **temperature** have been at 14.00 hours? ________

6. What is the **range** between the highest and lowest **temperatures?**________

7. What was the average **temperature**? ________

This is a jumble of calculator exercises. Watch the **signs** and **decimal points**!

8. 7 446 ÷ 51 = ________
9. 4 328 x 43 = ________
10. 17 642 - 16 426 = ________
11. 183 006 + 27 051 = ________
12. 9 240 ÷ 84 = ________
13. 6 430 x 72 = ________
14. 50% of 3 980 = ________
15. 25% of 7 872 = ________
16. 73% of 12 828 = ________
17. 0.5 x 938 = ________
18. 4 007 x 72 = ________
19. 73 912 + 537 068 = ________
20. 537 068 - 73 912 = ________
21. 93 504 ÷ 64 = ________
22. $\frac{1}{20}$ of 3 745 = ________
23. 196.5 x 4 = ________
24. 748.63 x 7 = ________
25. 0.92 x 83 = ________
26. 731.5 ÷ 4 = ________
27. Record the temperature every hour, beginning at 9.00am, until 2.00pm. Add the vertical scale then show the temperatures and make a graph.

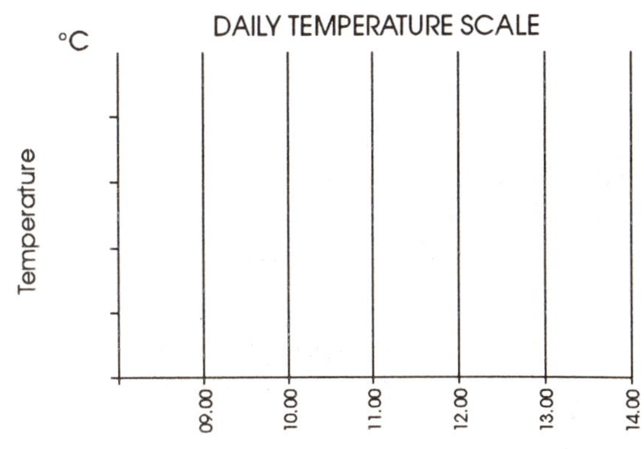

1. 32.4 + 28.6 = ______

2. 19.4 + 72.3 = ______

3. 27.5 + 46.9 = ______

4. 28.1 + 58.9 + 43.6 = ______

5. 19.2 + 36.9 + 48.3 + 26.5 = ______

6. 20.9 + 2.7 + 6.8 + 70.3 = ______

7. 63.4 + 48.9 + 97.1 = ______

8. 293.6 - 108.7 = ______

9. 603.3 - 533.9 = ______

10. 525.1 - 378.4 = ______

11. 406.4 - 327.8 = ______

12. 727.5 - 572.7 = ______

13. Erin walked **27.8km** to earn money for homeless children. Kate walked **21.6km.** What's the difference? ______

14. A boy had **£89.60** in the bank. He added **£25.40,** and then withdrew **£36.20.** What is the new bank balance? ______

15. Metered water is charged at **16.4** pence per kilolitre. When a lot is used the rate changes to **28.9** pence. What is the difference in pence per **kl?** ______

16. A small car uses **8.2l** of petrol per 100km. A truck uses **16.7l** per 100km. How much more does the truck use per 100km? ______

17. Petrol is sometimes measured in the 'old' imperial gallon measure. How many litres equal a gallon? ______

18. Tie and untie each of these **knots.** List situations were each **knot** could be used.

(a)

Thumb or overhand knot ______ ______

(b)

Double thumb-knot ______ ______

(c)

Figure-of-eight knot ______ ______

19. Make a **Möbius strip.** Take a piece of paper 3cm wide and 30cm long. Put a half twist in it and join the ends. Draw it.

20. Try to colour just one side of your **Möbius strip.** What do you notice?

______

______

21. Cut your **Möbius strip** down the centre and write about what happens.

______

______

22. Find out how the strip got its name.

______

______

Add these **decimal fractions.**

1. 7.83 + 16.01 + 3.96 = ______
2. 13.68 + 24.67 + 38.45 = ______
3. 17.1 + 6.84 + 35.5 + 9.08 = ______
4. 93.48 + 86.13 + 2.2 + 22.02 = ______
5. 86.39 + 1.07 + 0.62 + 38.4 = ______
6. 87.2 + 79.83 + 15.41 + 91.7 = ______

Subtract these **decimal fractions.**

7. 310.98 - 265.37 = ______
8. 267.8 - 130.04 = ______
9. 806.41 - 627.8 = ______
10. 984.5 - 23.79 = ______

11. In a race Donna recorded a time of **4 minutes 29.6 seconds.** Vanessa recorded a time of **4 minutes 23.8 seconds.** What is the difference? ______

12. A T-shirt is advertised at **£18. 65,** reduced from **£21.95.** What is the value of the reduction? ______

13. **1.35 litres** is poured from a **4.5l** bottle of cordial. How much is left in the bottle? ______

14. Engineers redesign a road so that instead of being **15.85km** long it will be **11.95km** long. What is the distance saved? ______

A gardener has to mow a lawn **100m x 50m.** He mows it in strips **lengthwise.** Each strip is **0.5 metres** wide.

15. How many times does he walk up and down? ______

16. Will he finish at the end where he started? ______

17. If he decided to mow the lawn crosswise, how many times would he walk up and down? ______

18. Mowing lengthwise, what distance will the gardener walk in kilometres? ______

19. Mowing crosswise, would there be any difference in distance? ______

20. What is the area of the lawn in hectares? ______

21. After mowing, the gardener spread fertilizer at the rate of **one kilogram per 10 square metres.** How much fertilizer did he use? ______

22. There is a pathway 1 metre wide all the way round the lawn. What is the area of the pathway? ______

23. £1274.39 + 619.03 + 4172.68 = ______
24. £2798.93 + 47.08 + 6773.97 = ______
25. £3126.25 - 477.89 = ______
26. £4296.61 - 177.78 = ______
27. £2781.51 - 1987.86 = ______
28. £3247.65 - 1798.77 = ______

1. Do some research on **credit cards** and list some you find.

____

____

____

____

____

2. **Credit card providers** make money by charging **interest** when payment is not made by the due date. Choose two cards and find out the interest rate charged.

Interest Rate

(a) _______________ _______________

(b) _______________ _______________

3. If the card holder makes full payment of the balance before the due date, will the **credit provider** still make money? How?

____

____

4. If you use a **credit card** while on an overseas trip in a number of countries, what happens about **rates of exchange?**

____

____

5. **Bartering** is a form of **cashless transaction.** How does **bartering** work?

____

____

____

6. Give an example of **bartering.**

____

____

7. Using a **pair of compasses** and a ruler, draw a circle with a **radius** of 3cm.

8. Draw a horizontal line across the circle, dividing it in two.

9. Mark on your drawing the *CENTRE, CIRCUMFERENCE, RADIUS* and *DIAMETER.*

10. What is the length of the **diameter?** _______

11. It is _______________ the **radius.**

12. Draw a second **diameter** at right angles to the one you have drawn.

13. What is the size of each of the four angles at the centre? _______

14. How many degrees when you add them all together? _______

15. Join the four points where the **diameters** meet the **circumference.**

16. What **2-D** shape have you drawn? _______________

17. How many **diameters** can you draw on a circle? _______

18. Does a **semi-circle** have a diameter? _____

1. Fill in the **digital** clocks to show the time it is now where you are, and what time it is in these places.

Where I am	Iceland	Brisbane
:	:	:
Brazil	**Canada (east coast)**	**USA (east coast)**
:	:	:
Canada (west coast)	**USA (west coast)**	**USA (Hawaii)**
:	:	:

2. What do you observe about the times above as you move east to west?

____

____

3. Why is **daylight saving** introduced in some places each summer?

____

____

4. During what months does daylight saving apply?

____

____

5. How long does it take the Earth to rotate 360°? _______

6. How many times does it do this in one year? _______

7. Does the moon rotate? _________

8. If it is 10.00a.m. in London, find out what time it is in:

(a) Singapore_______ (b) Bombay_______

(c) Cairo _______ (d) Rome _______

(e) Sydney _______ (f) New York _______

(g) Madrid _______ (h) Tokyo _______

9. Draw a circle with a **radius** of **4cm.**

10. Using a **protractor,** draw **radii** *(plural of radius)* at 45° **intervals** (45° apart).

11. Into how many parts did you divide the **circle?** _______

12. Join all the points where the **radii** meet the **circumference**. What **2-D** shape have you drawn? _______

13. What is meant by being **"in the red"?**

____

____

14. What is meant by being **"in the black"?**

____

____

15. What is the normal time difference between London and New York? _______

16. These are London 24 hour times. Fill in the New York times and days beneath.

London	0535	1857	0159
	Monday	Monday	Monday
New York			
	_______	_______	_______

1. Find out yesterday's **exchange rates** for the **pound** in these **currencies.**

Spain ______ U.S.A. ______

Germany ______ New Zealand ______

France ______ Japan ______

2. What is a **mortgage?**

______

______

______

3. Jade's parents have a **mortgage** of £95 000 on their home. The **interest** is £9 500 per year. What is this as a **percentage?** ______

4. At a furniture sale everything is reduced by **25%.** If you bought a table for **£300,** what was its price before the sale? ______

5. A racing bicycle is advertised at **£330,** with **$33\frac{1}{3}$%** off if you pay **cash.** How much would you need to buy the bicycle for **cash?** ______

6. Interest paid on a loan at **10%** came to **£400** over two years. How much was the loan? ______

7. What does **per annum** or **p.a.** mean?

______

8. A bank pays **5%** on the first **£1 000** and **6%** on the second **£1 000.** If you left **£2 000** with the bank for 2 years, how much interest would you earn? ______

9. Using a ruler and **protractor,** draw these triangles. Add the angles.

(a) Isosceles — Sum (total) of the angles ______

(b) Equilateral ______

(c) Right angle ______

(d) Scalene ______

10. What do you notice about the **sum** of the **angles?** ______

11. Draw these letters of the alphabet using a **protractor,** and mark all the angles in degrees. E Y.

12. On another sheet of paper, draw a piece of modern art with as many **2-D** shapes as you can think of, using a protractor and pair of compasses. Colour the picture and draw a frame around it.

1. Measure these lines in **millimetres.**

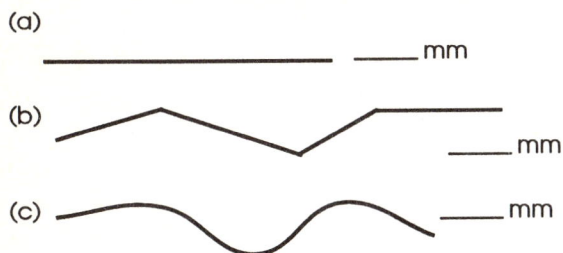

(a) ______ mm

(b) ______ mm

(c) ______ mm

2. Draw lines of these lengths from the points.

(a) 32mm
•

(b) 17mm
•

(c) 59mm
•

3. Write these lengths in **metres** to **three decimal places.**

(a) 935mm ______

(b) 2 183mm ______

(c) 7 046mm ______

(d) 1 110mm ______

4. Draw a circle with a **radius** of 25mm.

5. Draw two **diameters** at right angles so the circle is divided into quarters.

6. Measure a quarter of the **circumference** in millimetres. ______

7. What is the total **circumference** in mm? ______

8. A ———————————— B

(a) At point A draw a **45 millimetre** line downwards at **90°.** Mark the end of it C.

(b) Draw a line at **45°** from C so it meets B.

(c) How long is the line C to B in mm? ______

(d) What sort of triangle have you drawn? ______

(e) What is the sum of its angles? ______

9. Draw an **equilateral** triangle with sides **32mm.**

10. Complete the table.

mm	cm	m
	98	
		1.2
1 750		

11. You buy a computer game that is advertised for **£44,** but find there has been a 20% price increase. What is the new price? ______

12. A town's rainfall was **1 200mm** last year. This year it's already **1 440mm.** What is the percentage increase? ______

Unit 34

1.	2.	3.
4831	7821	94860
7629	84985	1902
3546	2798	40
+ 5283	+ 61349	+ 73425
______	______	______

4.	5.	6.
2786	78909	26413
68941	9787	8
3000	98078	5740
+ 95433	+ 8970	+ 58619
______	______	______

7. Picton has a population of **2 074,** Peak Hill has a population of **1 400** and Parkes has a population of **9 500.** What do the populations total? ______

8. What is the average population? ______

9. Mornington has a population of **27 397,** Pakenham **3 052** and Sunbury **15 297.** What do these populations total? ______

10. Average population? ______

The world's three longest rivers are the

Nile 6 670km (______________)

Amazon 6 437km (______________)

Mississippi
Missouri 6 231km (______________)

11. Add the lengths together. ______ km

12. In the brackets above write the continents in which these rivers are found.

Write the missing numbers.

13.	14.	15.
7896	3_46	27_
4_2	96_4	2_36
+ 3_17	+ _26_	+ _984
1_01_	16888	97_2

16. A rectangle measures **3cm x 4cm.** What is its **area?** ______

17. A square is **12cm x 12cm.** What is its **area?** ______

18. A rectangle is **42mm x 8mm.** What is its **area?** ______

19. A right angle triangle has two equal sides of **6cm.** What is its **area?** ______

20. How many **mm²** in **4cm²?** ______

21. Calculate these **areas.**

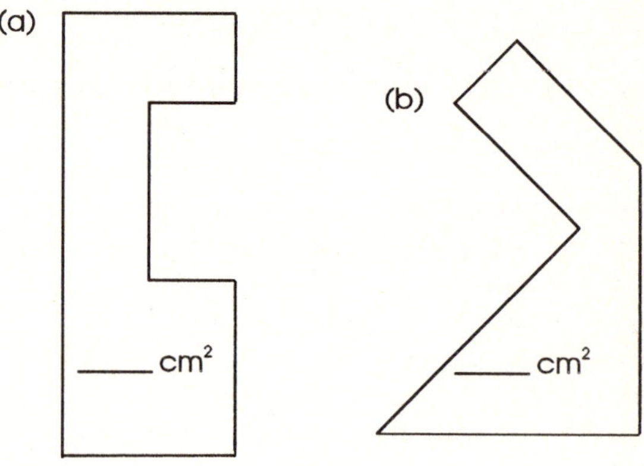

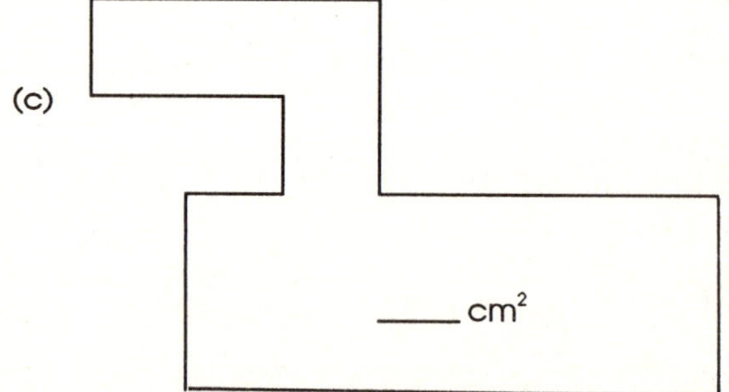

22. This is a plan of a playground drawn to a **scale of 1cm = 100m.** What is the **area** in square metres?

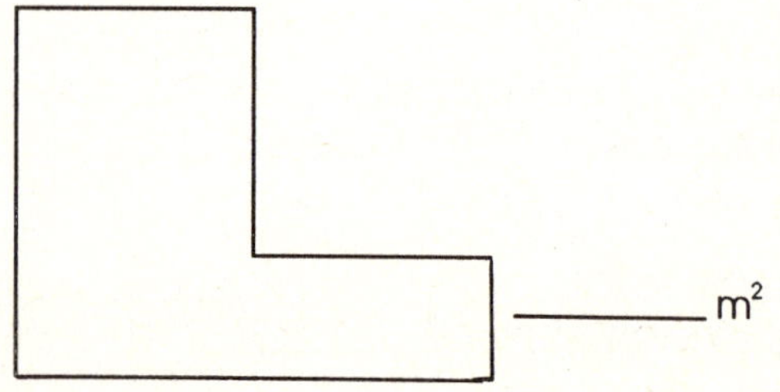

Add these sums of money.

1. £342.70 + 638.62 + 21.54 = ______
2. £789.92 + 541.83 + 256.05 = ______
3. £1338.11 + 6529.54 + 730.27 = ______
4. £7896.78 + 6823.56 + 3061.43 + 9873.58 = ______
5. £17804.34 + 8564.09 + 5241.72 + 76499.99 = ______

6. Find out how many days you have been alive. ______

7. A school's four best batsmen scored these runs in a season: **1 611, 1 274, 986** and **854.** How many runs for them altogether? ______

8. In an opinion poll, **13 746** people said they approved of the Prime Minister, **16 980** said they didn't and **4 092** people said they couldn't make up their minds. How many people were surveyed? ______

9. What is an opinion poll?

______

______

Four of the smaller states in the United States have these areas.

Vermont - 24 887km ^{2}
South Carolina - 80 432km ^{2}
New Hampshire - 24 097km ^{2}
New Jersey - 20 295km ^{2}

10. What is the combined area? ______

11. Florida has an area of 151 670km ^{2}. What is the difference in area between the four combined states and Florida? ______

12. Complete the addition sum and make up a story to go with it.

2 593 + 3 648 + 4 035 =

______

______

13. How many **centimetres** in **600mm?** ______

14. A rectangle is **33m x 49m.** What is it area? ______

15. A lawn measures **35m x 10m.** A garden **5m x 3m** is cut out of it. How much lawn remains? ______

16. A microwave oven is set for 4 minutes, but it stops when the digital clock shows **01:34.** For how long has it been cooking? ______

17. We each create one tonne of waste per year. How much waste would **600** people create in **3** months? ______

18. £19076.58 + 23148.29 + 264.13 + 1043.27 = ______
19. £36402.75 + 29.16 + 3128.53 + 80345.44 = ______
20. £27145.50 + 3007.19 + 40896.72 + 9354.07 = ______
21. £31268.17 + 7007.08 + 35.84 + 44041.33 = ______

22. Using a scale of **1cm = 100m** find the **area** of each shape in **hectares.**

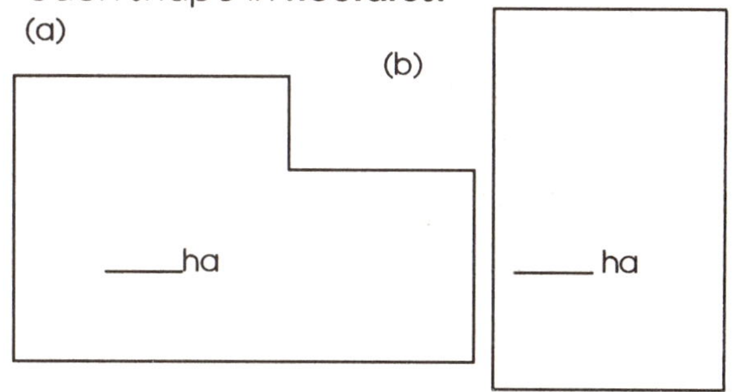

23. 63 847 + 25 176 + 3 875 = ______

24. Add three numbers to this sequence.

4 6 9 11 14 16 ___ ___ ___

1. Complete the **subtraction** number wheels.

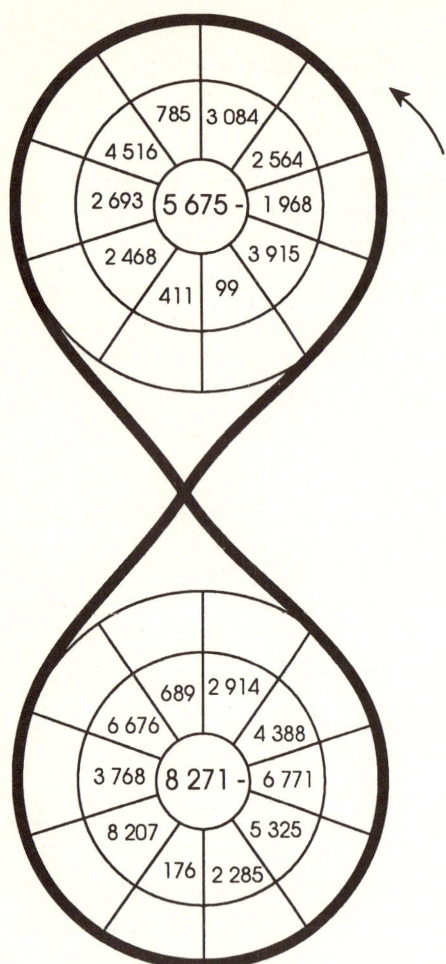

2. The number wheels are joined by a cross-over driving belt. The top wheel moves in the direction of the arrow. Show the direction the other wheel turns by drawing an arrow on it.

3. A canteen sold **3 781** soft drinks on Monday and **2 554** on Tuesday. What is the difference? ________

4. On Wednesday it sold **4 376** drinks. How many more than on Tuesday? ________

5. Complete the sum, then make up a story to go with it.

____

____

$$\begin{array}{r} 5000 \\ -3467 \\ \hline \\ \hline \end{array}$$

6. Add the rest of the **bearings (degrees)** to the compass.

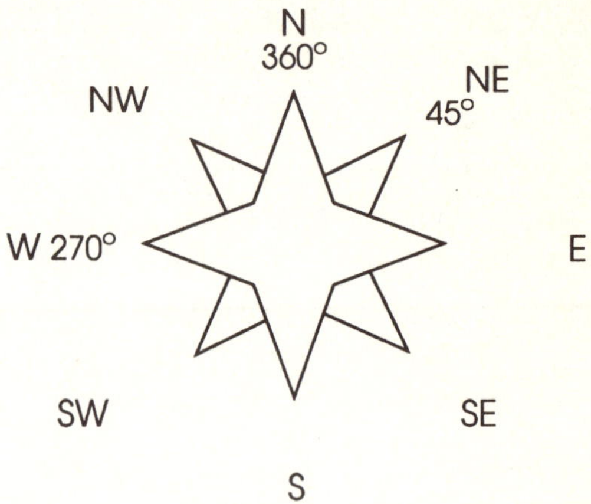

7. If you were in a boat and changed course from south to south-west, through how many degrees would you move? ________

8. If you changed from north-west to north, through how many degrees would you move? ________

9. How many degrees between south-east and south-west? ________

10. How many degrees between north-east and south-west? ________

11. Look at the **compass** above and without using a protractor, work out the bearings for

(a) ESE ________ (b) SSW ________

(c) WNW ________ (d) NNE ________

12. A ship on a course of 270° changes course 90° to starboard *(right)*. In which direction is it heading now? ________

13. An aircraft heading WSW has to return to the original airport. What will the new bearing be? ________

14. Do some research. What is a **compass rose?**

____

____

1. £2746.75 − 341.50 = ______

2. £3197.05 − 784.64 = ______

3. £8624.36 − 1925.74 = ______

4. £7092.47 − 6123.40 = ______

5. £9874.95 − 8947.59 = ______

6. £70416.35 − 9325.87 = ______

7. 397438 − 186549 = ______

8. 127419 − 119527 = ______

9. A mining town had a population of **3 741.** The mine closed down leaving only **1 946** people. How many left town? ______

10. A train stops for half a day **1 384km** on a **2 750km** journey. How much of the journey left to go? ______

11. Most communication satellites orbit the earth at a height of **35 000km.** Skylab reached a height of **435km** before exploding. How far short of orbit was it? ______

12. A busy hotel used **819 112l** of water on a hot day but only **643 730l** on the next day. What was the fall in water consumption? ______

13. Sound travels at **4 800km** per hour in water and **1 150km** per hour in the air. What is the difference in speed? ______

14. What is the opposite **direction** to North-North-East? ______

15. What is the opposite **direction** to West-North-West? ______

16. A ship is going west but changes course to SSW. How many **degrees** difference? ______

17. A walker is hiking NNW, but changes **course** 45° to the west. In what **direction** is she going? ______

18. 73491 − 29380 = ______

19. 433074 − 204963 = ______

20. 654318 − 473791 = ______

21. 765839 − 179696 = ______

22. £3340.79 − 1625.87 = ______

23. £8006.30 − 427.95 = ______

24. Write these numbers in Roman numerals.

(a) 7 ______ (b) 89 ______

(c) 120 ______ (d) 635 ______

(e) 1 401 ______ (f) 516 ______

25. Calculate the **perimeter** of each area.

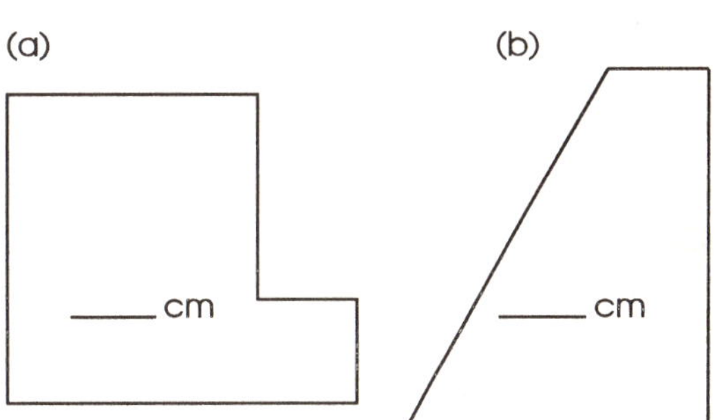

Do these calculations without using a calculator. Most involve moving the **decimal point.** The first one is done for you.

1. 1.3 x 10 = 13
2. 13 x 10 = ________
3. 3.13 x 10 = ________
4. 13.13 x 10 = ________
5. 0.6 x 100 = ________
6. 6.3 x 100 = ________
7. 3.68 x 100 = ________
8. 36.7 x 100 = ________
9. 3.78 x 100 = ________
10. 27.09 x 100 = ________
11. 13.96 x 1 = ________
12. 10.04 x 10 = ________
13. Each cashier at a large city bank has **£2 500** in their cash drawer when the bank opens. If there are **10** cashiers, how much money in the drawers altogether? ________
14. The average rainfall for Billings is **435.6mm** per year. What is the rainfall for **10** years? ________
15. The earth's **temperature** is said to be increasing at **0.05°C** every year. How much will the Earth's **temperature** increase in **100** years? ________
16. Try these more difficult calculations without using a calculator.

    (a) 22.75 x 100 = ________

    (b) 50.09 x 1 000 = ________

    (c) 7.4 x 1 000 = ________

Use a calculator for these.

17. 3.62 x 7 = ________
18. 9.03 x 8 = ________
19. 4.08 x 9 = ________
20. 5.96 x 5 = ________

21. Draw the ground plan of a house you would build on this land. Include in your house:

- Main living area
- Bathroom
- 2 bedrooms
- Utility room
- Kitchen
- Toilet
- Dining room
- Garage
- Patio

The road, north and the direction of the prevailing wind are shown.

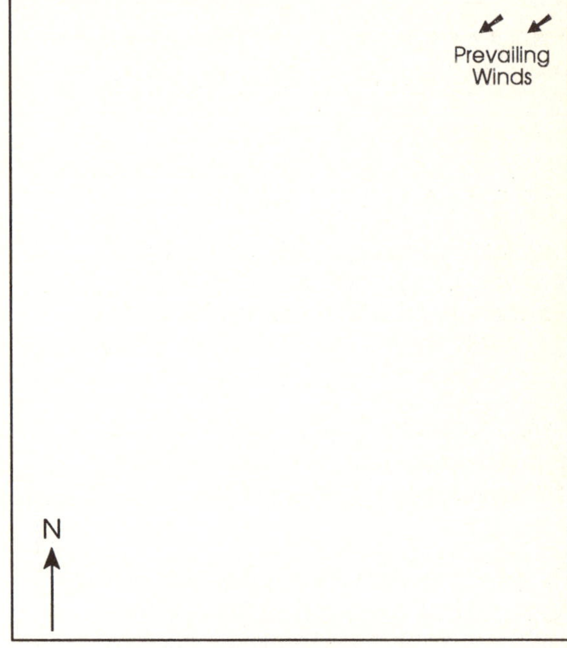

22. Start at the dot and using a ruler and protractor, plot this course.

NW 3cm → N 1cm → NNE 2cm → ESE 3cm
SW 2cm → ESE 3cm → SSE 1½cm → W 2cm

Start
Here ●

Find the **weight** of water each container will hold by first weighing the container empty, then when full. When you know the **weight** of water calculate the **capacity** of the container.

Container	Weight Empty	Weight Full	Weight of Water	Capacity
1. Cup				
2. Jug				
3. Cake tin				
4. Pie dish				
5. Saucepan				
6. Indoor watering can				

7. Complete these statements.

(a) 1 kg of water has a volume of _____ l

(b) 500ml = _____ l

(c) 15g of water = _____ ml

(d) 20cm^3 = _____ ml

(e) 0.5kg of water = _____ ml

(f) 2kl of water has a weight of _____ t

(g) 0.75l = _____ m^3

8. What unit of **capacity** would you use for a road tanker built to carry petrol or milk? _______

9. How much water do you think an eye dropper holds? _______

10. What is the **capacity** of an egg cup? _______

11. How many **millilitres** are contained in a thimble? _______

12. What is the **capacity** of a screw top lid? _______

Complete this plan of a theme park, using a **scale** of **1cm = 25m.**

13. What are the dimensions of the park? _______

14. What is the area of the park? _______

15. Describe where the entrance is.

____

____

16. Show these features on the plan.

(a) Big Dipper: 100m west of entrance

(b) Ghost Train: 75m south-west from north-east corner

(c) Dolphins: 75m south-west from Ghost Train

(d) Carousel: 75m NW of Big Dipper

(e) Big Wheel: 100m east from Carousel

(f) Water Slide: 60m SE from NW corner

(g) Computerland: 125m NW from entrance

(h) Snack bar: 75m south of NE corner

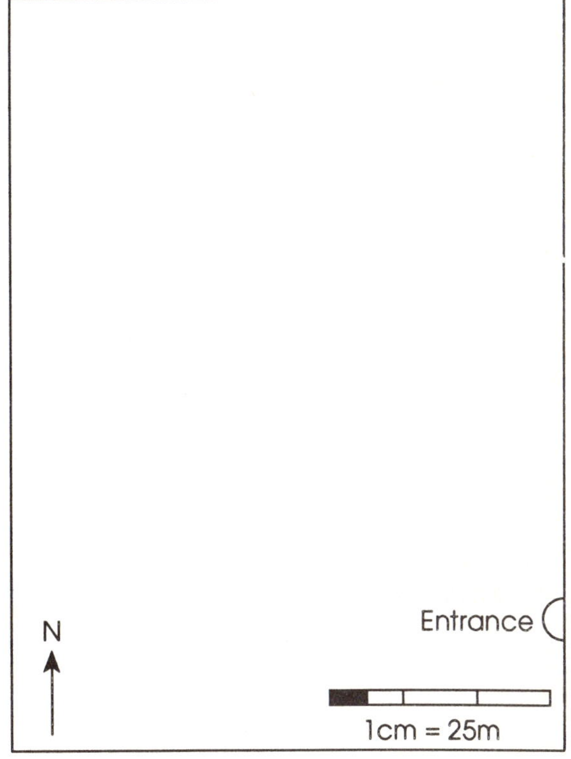

Unit 37

Use a calculator to do these **divisions**. Take the answer to two **decimal places** where necessary.

1. 16.8 ÷ 3 = ______ 2. 21.9 ÷ 7 = ______

3. 32.65 ÷ 5 = ______ 4. 29.06 ÷ 9 = ______

5. 16.78 ÷ 6 = ______ 6. 32.7 ÷ 4 = ______

7. £72 less 25% = ______

8. 33% off £166.50 = ______

9. An item normally priced at **£150** is included in a **40%** off sale. What is the **discount** price? ______

10. At a **fire** sale, a carpet that usually sells for **£160** is reduced to **£80.** What is the percentage discount? ______

11. An item is selling for **£40** and is **80%** of the usual price. What is the usual price? ______

Use a calculator to find the answers to these **division** sums. Write the answers to two **decimal places.**

12. $2\overline{)49.9}$

13. $4\overline{)31.65}$

14. $6\overline{)27.04}$

15. $5\overline{)24.36}$

16. $7\overline{)23.12}$

17. Money box savings of **£183.72** are to be shared equally among **4** children. How much does each receive? ______

18. How much left over? ______

This is a **pie chart** of the world's rice production.

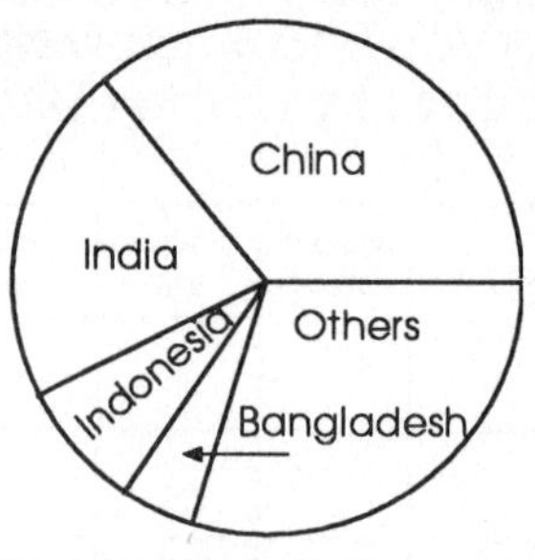

WORLD RICE PRODUCTION

19. List three countries that could be among the 'others'.

______

______

______

20. About how many times greater is India's rice production than Indonesia's? ______

21. China's rice production is about ______ that of India's.

22. Express Bangladesh's rice production as an approximate percentage of total world production. ______

23. Divide this pie chart into 24 parts and then show how you spend a normal school day. Include *sleeping, school, eating, travelling, playing* and *other.* Label and colour the slices.

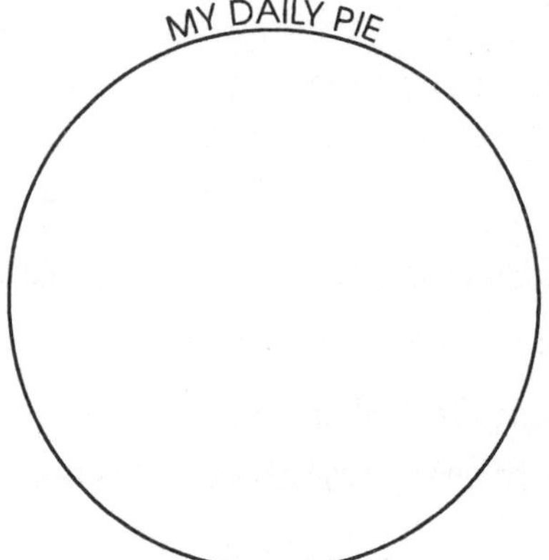

1. Find the **weight** in **tonnes** of a car or van in your family. ________

2. Find out the **weight** in **tonnes** of a bus. ________

3. What **tonnage** of oil does an ocean-going tanker carry? ________

4. What is the average **weight** of an adult male? ________

5. What is the average **weight** of an adult female? ________

6. Combine the two weights above to find the **weight** of an average adult. ________

7. What would be the **weight** of 300 adults travelling on an airliner? Give your answer in **tonnes.** ________

8. If each passenger's luggage averaged 40 kilograms, how many **tonnes** of luggage? ________

9. Convert these **weights** to **tonnes.**

(a) 1 750kg ________

(b) 19 020kg ________

(c) 480kg ________

(d) 36 163kg ________

10. Find out about 'old ' measures of weight like pounds and stones.

(a) How many pounds in a stone? ________

(b) A newborn baby weighs 3kg. About how many pounds does the baby weigh? ________

11. 25% of 300 = ______ 12. 50% of 760 = ______

13. 15% of 400 = ______ 14. $\frac{1}{3}$ of 630 = ______

15. $\frac{2}{3}$ of 900 = ______ 16. 80% of 720 = ______

17. Write $\frac{2}{3}$ as a **percentage.** ______

18. What is 16.66% as a **fraction?** ______

19. What is $33\frac{1}{3}$% as a **fraction?** ______

20. 75% of 200 = ______ 21. 60% of 500 = ______

22. Convert these **kilograms** to **tonnes.**

(a) 2 789kg ________

(b) 14 806kg ________

(c) 9 960kg ________

23. Convert these **tonnes** to **kilograms.**

(a) 152t ________

(b) 9.56t ________

(c) 11.01t ________

24. What is the average of **146, 209, 301** and **192?** ________

25. A car travels **900km** in **18** hours. What is the car's average speed? ________

Write the answers to these **division sums** to **two decimal places.**

26. 12) 837.9 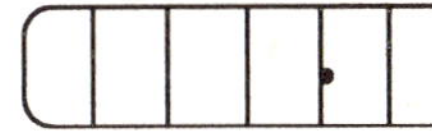

27. 19) 479.4 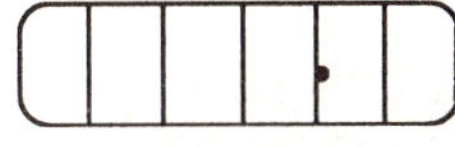

28. 13) 1 127.9 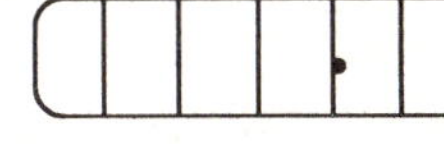

Unit 38

1. A family has paid off **£12 500** of a **£47 000 mortgage.** How much still to pay? _______

2. For four years they only paid the **interest** at **9.75%.** What does the **interest** amount to? _______

3. A **credit card** statement shows that **£397** is owing. The **'due date'** is passed and a month's **interest** is to be added at **1.65%.** What is now owed? _______

4. A woman earning **£381** per week receives a **15%** pay rise. What is her new weekly wage? _______

5. A warehouse is advertised for rent at **£3 per square metre** per month. If the warehouse is **1 200m²**, what is the monthly rent? _______

6. An estate agent advertises two houses for sale as an investment. Good tenants. **£134 000.** Return **8.5%** per year. What would the new owner earn from rents? _______

7. List the names of five big companies and what their shares were worth yesterday.

Companies	Share Value

8. If you owned **1 000** shares in each company what would be the total value of your shares? _______

This **graph** shows the number of children enrolled at a school over ten years.

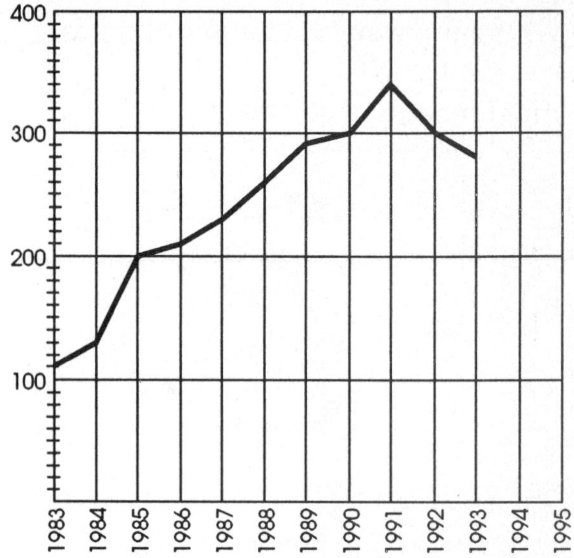

9. What was the enrolment in 1983? _______

10. What was the enrolment in 1988? _______

11. In what year did the enrolments peak? _______

12. In which year was the enrolment twice that of 1984? _______

13. Which was the first year to show a drop in enrolments? _______

14. How many girls were enrolled in 1986, if there are about equal numbers of boys and girls at the school? _______

15. Continue the graph and predict the enrolments for 1994 and 1995.

1994: _______ 1995: _______

The school has one teacher for every 25 pupils.

16. How many teachers were on staff in 1988? _______

17. How many teachers in 1991? _______

18. What is your prediction for 1994? _______

1. Draw on this map the International Date Line, the Equator and Tropics of Cancer and Capricorn. Label each one.

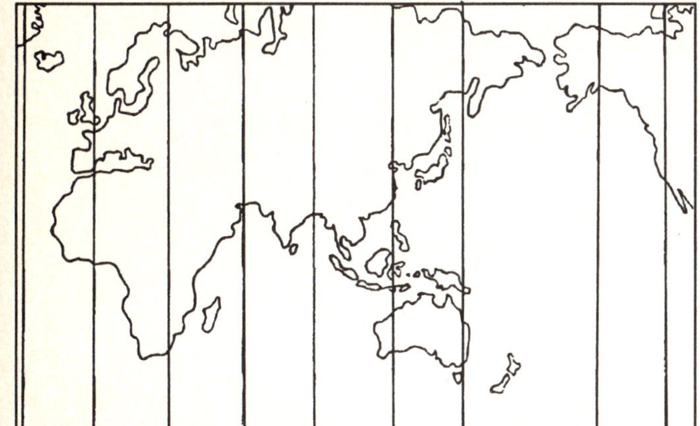

2. What does **equinox** mean? ______________

____

3. What does **solstice** mean? ______________

____

4. On what date is our **summer solstice?** __________

5. What is **Greenwich Mean Time?**

____

____

____

6. Perth time is two hours earlier than Sydney time, and London time is ten hours earlier than Sydney time.

(a) What time is it in Perth when it's 10 a.m. in Sydney? ______

(b) What time is it in London when it is 3.00 p.m. in Sydney? ______

(c) What time is it in London when it is 11.00 a.m. in Perth? ______

(d) What time and day is it in London when it is 8.00 a.m. on Tuesday in Sydney?

______________ __________

(e) What time and day is it in Perth when it is 1 a.m. on Sunday in Sydney?

______________ __________

7. What is the **share** or **stock market?**

____

____

8. What is a **sharebroker** or **stockbroker?**

____

____

9. A sum of £25 000 earns 6.5% p.a. What interest is this in one year? ______

10. How many years to earn **£3 250** at the same rate? ______

11. It is midday in England and England are playing Australia in a cricket match. TV viewers watch the match in Sydney, Australia. What time is it in Sydney? ______

12.
```
  £3182.76
   3451.78
 +  967.25
 _________
```

13.
```
  £4783.91
  -3694.05
 _________
```

14.
```
  907.8
  x   9
 ______
```

15. 7) 84.56

16. 104.7 x 6 = ______ 17. 974 x 21 = ______

18. Continue this sequence.

1 2 3 3 6 4 10 5 ____ ____ ____

19. What year is the Roman numeral **MCMVIII**? ______

20. 25% of £2 400 = ____

21. What is the value of the third angle in each triangle. Remember, all add to 180°.

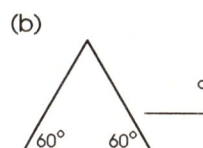

(a)

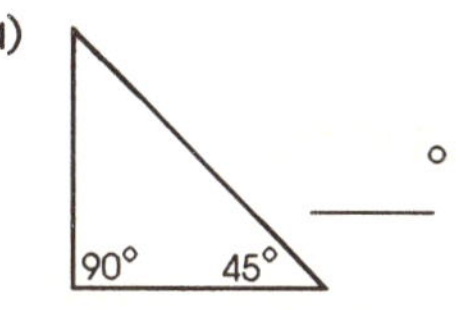

____°

(b)

60° 60°

____°

Useful Facts

Roman Numerals

1	2	3	4	5	6	7	8	9	10
I	II	III	IV	V	V1	VII	VIII	IX	X

20	30	40	50	60	90	100
XX	XXX	XL	L	LX	XC	C

200	400	500	900	1 000
CC	CD	D	CM	M

Compass Points

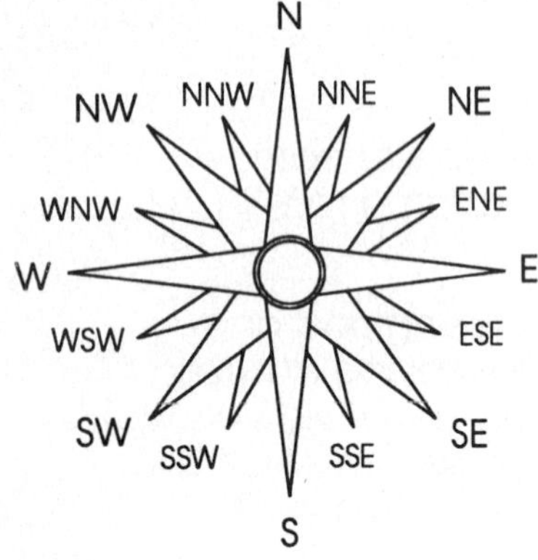

Formulae

Area of a
rectangle = L x W (length x width)

Volume of a rectangular
prism = L x W x H (length x width x height)

Area of a
triangle = $\frac{1}{2}$ B x H (Half base x height)

Percentages	Fractions	Decimals
5%	$\frac{1}{20}$	0.05
10%	$\frac{1}{10}$	0.1
25%	$\frac{1}{4}$	0.25
50%	$\frac{1}{2}$	0.5
75%	$\frac{3}{4}$	0.75
$33\frac{1}{3}\%$	$\frac{1}{3}$	0.333
$66\frac{2}{3}\%$	$\frac{2}{3}$	0.666
$16\frac{2}{3}\%$	$\frac{1}{6}$	0.166
$12\frac{1}{2}\%$	$\frac{1}{8}$	0.125
$37\frac{1}{2}\%$	$\frac{3}{8}$	0.375
$62\frac{1}{2}\%$	$\frac{5}{8}$	0.625

Measurement

10mm = 1cm
1cm^3 of water has a weight of 1g
1l of water has a weight of 1kg
1 000kg = 1 tonne (t)

Capacity

1 000 millilitres (ml) = 1 litre (l)
The weight of 1 millilitre of water is 1 gram
1 000 grams (g) = 1 kilogram (kg)
1 litre of water has a weight of 1 kilogram
1 000 000 cubic centimetres = 1 cubic metre (m^3)

Area

100 square millimetres = 1 cm^2
10 000 square centimetres = 1 m^2
10 000 square metres = 1ha
1 000 000 square metres = 1km^2
100 hectares = 1km^2

Angles

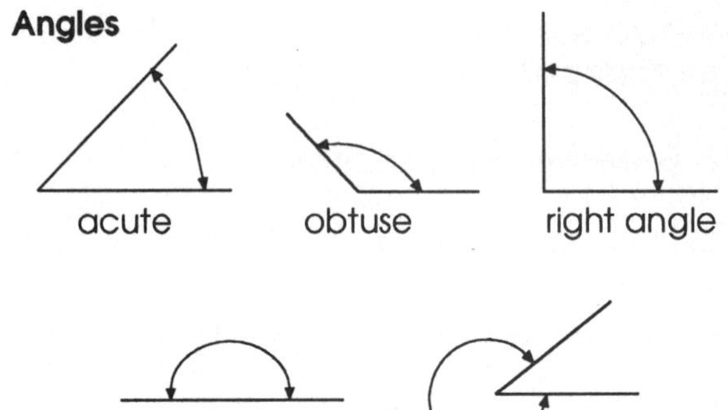

The angles of a triangle add up to 180°.
There are 360° in a circle.

Numbers

1 634 728 - One million six hundred and thirty-four thousand seven hundred and twenty-eight

78 795 021 - Seventy-eight million seven hundred and ninety-five thousand and twenty-one

465 310 702 - Four hundred and sixty-five million three hundred and ten thousand seven hundred and two

Time

When writing B.C. or A.D. always place B.C. after the year (536 B.C.); always place A.D. before the year (A.D. 1925).